# Lecture Notes
# in Business Information Processing     38

## Series Editors

Wil van der Aalst
*Eindhoven Technical University, The Netherlands*

John Mylopoulos
*University of Trento, Italy*

Norman M. Sadeh
*Carnegie Mellon University, Pittsburgh, PA, USA*

Michael J. Shaw
*University of Illinois, Urbana-Champaign, IL, USA*

Clemens Szyperski
*Microsoft Research, Redmond, WA, USA*

Raúl Poler  Marten van Sinderen
Raquel Sanchis (Eds.)

# Enterprise Interoperability

Second IFIP WG 5.8 International Workshop, IWEI 2009
Valencia, Spain, October 13-14, 2009
Proceedings

Volume Editors

Raúl Poler
Raquel Sanchis
Polytechnic University of Valencia
Research Centre on Production Management and Engineering
Camino de Vera s/n, Ed. 8G – $1^a$ y $4^a$ Planta Acc. D
(Ciudad Politécnica de la Innovación), 46022 Valencia, Spain
E-mail: {rpoler,rsanchis}@cigip.upv.es

Marten van Sinderen
University of Twente
Centre for Telematics and Information Technology
PO Box 217, 7500 AE Enschede, The Netherlands
E-mail: m.j.vansinderen@ewi.utwente.nl

Library of Congress Control Number: 2009935340

ACM Computing Classification (1998): J.1, H.3.5, D.2.12

ISSN       1865-1348
ISBN-10    3-642-04749-1 Springer Berlin Heidelberg New York
ISBN-13    978-3-642-04749-7 Springer Berlin Heidelberg New York

springer.com

© IFIP International Federation for Information Processing 2009
Printed in Germany

Typesetting: Camera-ready by author, data conversion by Scientific Publishing Services, Chennai, India
Printed on acid-free paper     SPIN: 12762880     06/3180     5 4 3 2 1 0

# Preface

One of the trends in the global market is the increasing collaboration among enterprises. Constant changes in inter- and intra-organizational environments will persist in the future. Organizations have to flexibly and continuously react to (imminent) changes in markets and trading partners. Large companies but also SMEs have to cope with internal changes from both a technical (e.g., new information, communication, software and hardware technologies) and an organizational point of view (e.g., merging, re-organization, virtual organizations, etc.). In this context, the competitiveness of an enterprise depends not only on its internal performance to produce products and services, but also on its ability to seamlessly interoperate with other enterprises. External and internal collaborative work needs more interoperable solutions.

The International Workshop on Enterprise Interoperability, IWEI, aims at identifying and discussing challenges and solutions with respect to enterprise interoperability, both at the business and the technical level. The workshop promotes the development of a scientific foundation for specifying, analyzing and validating interoperability solutions; an architectural framework for addressing interoperability problems from different viewpoints and at different levels of abstraction; a maturity model to evaluate and rank interoperability solutions with respect to distinguished quality criteria; and a working set of practical solutions and tools that can be applied to interoperability problems to date.

IWEI is organized by the IFIP Working Group 5.8 on Enterprise Interoperability. The aim of IFIP WG5.8 is to advance and disseminate research and development results in the area of enterprise interoperability. The IWEI workshop therefore provides a platform where ideas that have emerged from IFIP WG5.8 meetings can be discussed, or reversely, where issues raised at the workshop can be taken to the IFIP community for further contemplation and investigation.

This volume contains the proceedings of the second workshop, IWEI 2009, held October 13–14, 2009, in Valencia, Spain. Eleven papers were selected for oral presentation and publication, based on a thorough review process, in which each paper was reviewed by three experts in the field. The papers are representative of the current research activities in the area of enterprise interoperability. The papers cover a wide range of Enterprise Interoperability issues from foundational theories, frameworks, architectures, methods and guidelines to European project results and case studies.

We would like to take this opportunity to express our gratitude to all those who contributed to the IWEI 2009 workshop. We thank the authors for submitting content, which resulted in valuable information exchange and stimulating discussions; we thank the reviewers for providing useful feedback to the submitted content, which undoubtedly helped the authors to improve their work; and we thank the attendants for expressing interest in the content and initiating relevant discussions. We are indebted to IFIP TC5 for recognizing the importance of enterprise interoperability as a research area with high economic impact, and acting accordingly with the establishment of WG5.8. Finally, we are grateful to the Polytechnic University of Valencia for hosting the workshop.

October 2009                                                    Raul Poler
                                                    Marten van Sinderen
                                                    Raquel Sanchis

# Organization

IWEI 2009 was organized by the Research Centre on Production Management and Engineering (CIGIP) of the Polytechnic University of Valencia in cooperation with Centre for Telematics and Information Technology (CTIT) of the University of Twente.

## Executive Committee

Conference Chair            Raul Poler (CIGIP, Spain)
Program Chair               Marten van Sinderen (CTIT, The Netherlands)
Organizing Chair            Raquel Sanchis (CIGIP, Spain)

## Program Committee

Ricardo Chalmeta            University of Jaume I, Spain
David Chen                  Université Bordeaux 1, France
Paul Davidsson              Blekinge Institute of Technology, Sweden
Guy Doumeingts              INTEROP-VLab/GFI, France
Yves Ducq                   Université Bordeaux 1, France
Ricardo Goncalves           New University of Lisbon, UNINOVA, Portugal
Pontus Johnson              Royal Institute of Technology, Sweden
Leonid Kalinichenko         Russian Academy of Sciences, Russian Federation
Stephan Kassel              University of Applied Sciences Zwickau, Germany
Kurt Kosanke                CIMOSA Association, Germany
Lea Kutvonen                University of Helsinki, Finland
Francisco Cruz Lario        Polytechnic University of Valencia, Spain
Kai Mertins                 Fraunhofer IPK, Germany
Angel Ortiz                 Polytechnic University of Valencia, Spain
Paul Oude Luttighuis        Novay, The Netherlands
Hervé Panetto               Research Centre for Automatic Control University of Nancy, France
Dick Quartel                Novay, The Netherlands
Sven-Volker Rehm            University of Stuttgart and the Otto Beisheim School of Management, Germany
Pierre-Yves Schobbens       University of Namur, Belgium
Marten Schönherr            Technische Universität Berlin, Germany
Markus Strohmaier           Graz University of Technology, Austria
Bruno Vallespir             Université Bordeaux 1, France
Alain Wegmann               Ecole Polytechnique Federal de Lausanne, Switzerland
Xiaofei Xu                  Harbin Institute of Technology, China

## Sponsoring Organizations

IFIP TC5 WG5.8
INTEROP-VLab
Centre for Telematics and Information Technology
Research Centre on Production Management and Engineering
Polytechnic University of Valencia
Spanish Ministry of Science and Innovation (Ref. TIN2009-06348-E/TSI)

# Table of Contents

## Full Papers

Towards Cross-Organizational Innovative Business Process
Interoperability Services ........................................ 1
    *Ömer Karacan, Enrico Del Grosso, Cyril Carrez, and
Francesco Taglino*

Barriers to Enterprise Interoperability ............................ 13
    *Johan Ullberg, David Chen, and Pontus Johnson*

A SOA-Based Platform-Specific Framework for Context-Aware Mobile
Applications..................................................... 25
    *Laura M. Daniele, Eduardo Silva, Luís Ferreira Pires, and
Marten van Sinderen*

An Ontological Solution to Support Interoperability in the Textile
Industry ....................................................... 38
    *Arantxa Duque, Cristina Campos, Ernesto Jiménez-Ruiz, and
Ricardo Chalmeta*

An Approach towards Enterprise Interoperability Assessment .......... 52
    *Mahsa Razavi and Fereidoon Shams Aliee*

Classifying Enterprise Architecture Analysis Approaches .............. 66
    *Sabine Buckl, Florian Matthes, and Christian M. Schweda*

Guiding the Service Engineering Process: The Importance of Service
Aspects......................................................... 80
    *Qing Gu, Patricia Lago, and Elisabetta Di Nitto*

From Business Value Model to Coordination Process Model ........... 94
    *Hassan Fatemi, Marten van Sinderen, and Roel Wieringa*

## Position Papers

SOP⁴EBPM: Generating Executable Business Services from Business
Models ........................................................ 107
    *Rubén de Juan-Marín and Rubén Darío Franco*

A Framework for a Decision Support System in a Hierarchical Extended
Enterprise Decision Context .................................... 113
    *Andrés Boza, Angel Ortiz, Eduardo Vicens, and Raul Poler*

An Interoperability Architecture for Networked Service Delivery ....... 125
  *Stephan Kassel, Christian-Andreas Schumann, Andreas Rutsch, and
  Thomas Reich*

**Author Index** ................................................... 133

# Towards Cross-Organizational Innovative Business Process Interoperability Services

Ömer Karacan[1], Enrico Del Grosso[2], Cyril Carrez[3], and Francesco Taglino[4]

[1] Siemens AG, Vienna, Austria
oemer.karacan@siemens.com
[2] TXT e-Solutions, Milano, Italy
enrico.delgrosso@txt.it
[3] SINTEF ICT, Oslo, Norway
Cyril.Carrez@sintef.no
[4] CNR-IASI, Roma, Italy
francesco.taglino@iasi.cnr.it

**Abstract.** This paper presents the vision and initial results of the COIN (FP7-IST-216256) European project for the development of open source Collaborative Business Process Interoperability (CBPip) in cross-organisational business collaboration environments following the Software-as-a-Service Utility (SaaS-U) paradigm.

**Keywords:** Interoperability, business, collaborative process, COIN.

## 1 Introduction

COIN (FP7-216256) [1] is an integrated project in the European Commission Seventh Framework Programme. The mission of the COIN project is to study, design, develop and prototype an open, self-adaptive, generic ICT solution where Enterprise Collaboration (EC) and Enterprise Interoperability (EI) services will be an invisible, pervasive and self-adaptive knowledge and business utility at the disposal of the European networked enterprises [13].

In this paper we position the vision and initial results for the development of open source Collaborative Business Process Interoperability (CBPip) services following the Software-as-a-Service Utility (SaaS-U) paradigm. SaaS is a model of software deployment where an application is hosted as a service provided to customers across the Internet, while SaaS-U brings in the picture a new field of interoperability among collaborative enterprises, hence SaaS becomes a utility for them.

The Collaborative Business process (CBP) interoperability is here meant to support cross organizational BP modelling by means of sharing, publishing, and transforming existing business process models.

This paper is structured as follows:

- In section 2 we give a short overview of related work and the context of the CBPip.
- Section 3 describes the prerequisites and concepts for implementing a first set of CBPip services.

R. Poler, M. van Sinderen, and R. Sanchis (Eds.): IWEI 2009, LNBIP 38, pp. 1–12, 2009.

- In section 4 we discuss how the CBPip services fit with the SaaS-U paradigm.
- Section 5 describes the status quo of the ongoing activities and preliminary results.
- Conclusions and future work are presented in section 6.

## 2  Related Work

The mission of COIN is to study, design, develop and prototype an open, self-adaptive, generic ICT integrated solution, starting from notable existing research results in the field of Enterprise Interoperability (specially ATHENA [3], and SHAPE [4]) and Enterprise Collaboration (specially ECOLEAD [2]).

In particular, a COIN business-pervasive open-source service platform will be able to expose, integrate, compose and mash-up in a secure and adaptive way existing and innovative to-be developed Enterprise Interoperability and Enterprise Collaboration services, by applying intelligent maturity models, business rules and self-adaptive decision-support guidelines to guarantee the best combination of the needed services in dependence of the business context, as industrial sector and domain, size of the companies involved, openness and dynamics of collaboration. This way, the Information Technology vision of Software as a Service (SaaS) will find its implementation in the field of interoperability among collaborative enterprises, supporting the various collaborative business forms, from supply chains to business ecosystems, and becoming for them like a utility, a commodity, the so-called Interoperability Service Utility (ISU)[24].

The COIN project will finally develop an original business model based on the SaaS-U paradigm where the open-source COIN service platform will be able to integrate both free-of-charge and chargeable, open and proprietary services depending on the case and business policies.

## 3  Collaborative Business Process Interoperability

The work in CBPip starts with the consolidation of open source results from the previous Enterprise Interoperability research, in particular the ATHENA project (FP6-507849) [3]. The ATHENA project was the integrated project focusing on enterprise interoperability in FP6. The project developed an interoperability framework baseline with a set of models, tools, services and methods to solve interoperability issues.

The work in CBPip inherits the results of the ATHENA project as prerequisites and introduces innovative enhancements, particularly business process interoperability according to SaaS-U paradigm.

There are two main CBPip project threads to develop the innovative enhancements. The first thread aims to develop innovative Collaborative Business Process Interoperability (CBPip) web services for business process modeling, semantic annotation and mediation, in order to allow a (semi-) automatic reconciliation between enterprise private processes (PP) and their public views, so-called view processes (VP). The ATHENA CBP approach helps us to define a procedure for low-level approach to design the CBP independently and for high-level approach to allow participants to expose to collaboration the view processes of their private processes and to let the CBP to be built interactively. It helps us to conceptualize the top-down Vertical Business Process Interoperability (VBPI) strategy.

The second thread of CBPiP aims to study and experiment process and workflow mining techniques to implement a vertical, bottom-up approach to align the business process interoperability models with the execution traces; the bottom-up Vertical Business Process Interoperability (VBPI) strategy.

## 3.1 Top-Down Vertical Business Process Interoperability

This section outlines the specification of an open source top-down Vertical Business Process Interoperability Services Framework. It takes the ATHENA CBP approach as a starting point and extends it with new novel approaches and EI services, offered as (Semantic) Web services and GUI front-ends (rich clients) according to SaaS and SaaS-U, to support Business Interoperability between collaborating Small Medium Enterprises (SME).

Figure 1 gives a high-level overview of the CBP approach. The different levels on which CBP modeling is performed (business level, technical level, implementation level) are represented on the vertical axis. On the horizontal axis the different model types of the process view concept are shown.

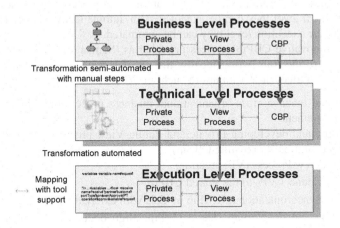

**Fig. 1.** High-level overview of CBP concepts

The different process levels are:

- Business level processes: This level represents the business views on the collaborative activities, and describes the cross organisational process that defines the interaction among the partners. The CBPs modelled on this level are destined for understanding and governance, and will not in the short term support execution.

- Technical level processes: This level provides a more detailed view on the CBP representing a more complete control flow of the process. Non-executable tasks are replaced by tasks that can be executed in a system; still the control flow is specified in a platform independent manner. This supports reuse of the process models as the models on this level can then be ported to different process engines on the last level. Also the message exchange between single tasks is modelled on this level.

- Execution level processes: On this level the CBP is modelled in the modelling language of a concrete business process engine. It is extended with platform specific interaction information and data, e.g. the concrete message formats sent or received during CBP execution or the specification of particular data sources providing data during process execution.

These levels are similar to the different types of models used in OMG model-driven architecture [5], namely computational independent models (CIM), platform independent models (PIM) and platform specific models (PSM). BPMN [6] (possibly extended with some CBP concepts) as a language can be used at the CIM level to express business process models or PIM models to express workflow models that can be (semi)automated and transformed to platform technologies. BPEL [12] is an execution process language that can be used at the PSM level.

At each intersection of a vertical and horizontal axis, we can identify a possible process model to capture tasks and relationships of cross-organizational interactions. Thus it is ensured that all relevant perspectives on CBP models as well as the processes required for the view concept are properly captured and modelled. Transformations between the different modeling levels are necessary. Between the business level and the technical level they can be executed semi-automatically, between the technical level and the execution level they can be automated.

A set of innovative CBPip services provided as (Semantic) Web Services will be the main part of the framework. Ideally, the set of services will need to support the complete CBPip lifecycle. Examples of such services are:

- Set up and manage cross-organizational business process in a shared collaborative environment.
- Modelling and developing Private and Public View processes (as part of the internal preparation for creating CBPip):
  - View Process (VP) creation.
  - Connect VPs to the shared CBPip.
  - Synchronization of CBPip models with external views.
- Modelling and developing shared CBPip: align document exchange in CBPip process parts.
- Execution of the CBPip, i.e., model transformations to executable platforms must be provided.
- Post-execution analysis of modelled CBPip.
- Infrastructure services for storing and executing the CBPip and their corresponding executables.
- Management and monitoring of CBPip.

These services can be used by either:

- Existing and commercial tools of the collaborating SMEs
- GUI front-ends developed as client-side prototypes as an alternative to existing/commercial tools (where these cannot be used or extended)

In COIN we will aim at leveraging existing technologies and extending them to support additional research issues. For instance, how to accommodate and integrate human-centric processes, e.g., at a PIM-level with BPEL for humans as a target platform. Another extension would focus on how semantic annotations/process models can help us, e.g., can semantic models help us automatically create view processes?

### 3.2 Bottom-Up Vertical Business Process Interoperability

The CBP modelling according to ATHENA is naturally focusing on business processes and collaborative business process modelling on a higher level – on the level CIM of OMG MDA [9], since they are the basic means of negotiation and communication to reach successful business collaboration. They address how to realize a business goal incorporating business information, business organizations, business partners and business resources (both human and machine). It is a logical step to describe CBP through business process modelling. However, in the CBP, the cross-organizational business process interoperability on the CIM, PIM and PSM levels (e.g. BPMN, SoaML [11] and BPEL respectively) is not the focus; the process interoperability is taken as prerequisite, if not, it is assumed as existing. The CBPip concept handles the business process interoperability conceptually through the introduction of the concept pairs "private process / view process". The view process is a derivation of a specific private process hiding the company's critical information from unauthorized partners: it will represent only the required information for external operations, while hiding internal aspects of the (private) process. A view process is always referenced to its private process, which assures business process interoperability. Figure 2 illustrates the difference between a view process and a private process, and how they are used in the COIN environment. Each company (A and B) build their own private processes, shown at the bottom of the figure. Using the COIN services (see section 5), each company will specify which parts of their processes they wish to publish, and then transform each process into a View Process, which will then be published in the COIN process repository. As shown on the figure, this View Process contains less operations and sub-processes than the Private Process. View Processes are then composed in the CBPip (upper part of Figure 2).

Additionally, the CBPip provides a modelling technique for studying and illustrating (modelling) business process interoperability challenges (problems and possible solutions), generally, on different levels of abstraction: the CBPip Modeling (CBPipM). The CBPipM offers a unified "look & feel" in all abstraction levels. This will drive us to define potential interoperability services and service utilities in respect to configuration, customization, testability, simulation (e.g. annotating ontologies, generating interoperability rules and mapping functions) and interoperability reverse engineering alias backward transformation (bottom-up strategy).

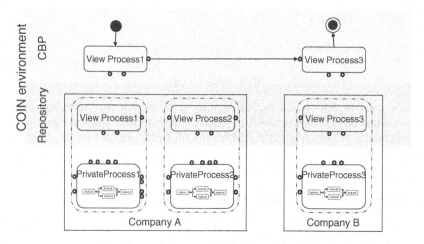

**Fig. 2.** Private Process and View Process in the COIN environment

Furthermore, CBPipM leverages the artefacts that are undergone a semantic compatibility procedure, where semantic annotation and semantic mediation services are performed.

The concept of CBPipM provides modelling means, where business process interoperability can be defined and modelled from different views and aspects, particularly in the PIM and PSM levels. The CBPipM enables behavioural examination of the CBP from the viewpoint of its interoperability as a whole. In other words, it describes and illustrates the "interoperability view" of CBP models.

The CBPipM is a complementary modelling approach for the ATHENA CBP modelling. Its premises are:

- The CBPipM is not a new modelling notation, but a modelling concept, which may be realized by extending (through profiling) the state-of-the-art modelling notations, e.g. BPMN, SoaML.
- The CBPipM models use the business logic and semantics already captured in CBP models but do not redefine them.
- The CBPipM is applicable in a semantically integrated, unified, or federated environment.
- The CBPipM focuses solely on business process interoperability modelling in a strong relationship to CBP models.
- The CBPipM model elements are definable by using CBP meta-model elements.
- The CBPipM suppresses business process centric model information (visualisation).
- The CBPipM supports vertical top-down (CIM -> PIM -> PSM -> IM) and bottom-up model transformations.

The CBPipM introduces the following modelling elements:

- state object
    - A model stereotype for the process data.
- Trans-operation and trans-mapping

    o    Model stereotypes for the interaction incorporating the transactions, particularly between View Process / Private Process pairs. Trans-operations are actions between COIN workflows and workflows of partner organization. Trans-mappings are co-local actions, i.e. they are not cross-organizational transactions. They are to be used particularly for semantic compatibility through invoking COIN semantic mediation services.

Using the state objects, trans-operations, and trans-mappings any cross-organization business interoperability workflow can be illustrated completely.

Figure 3 illustrate the relationship between a common CBP model and a CBPipM model. Note that, a fully automated M2M transformation from CBP model to CBPipM should be possible in the modelling environment.

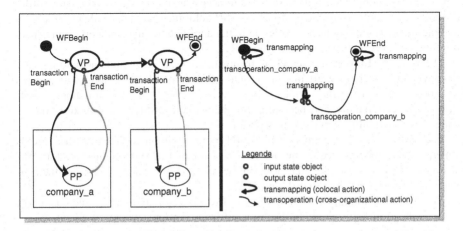

**Fig. 3.** CBP model vs. CBPip model

## 4    Towards EI Service Utilities

The COIN software model is built on software-as-a-service (SaaS) and software-as-a-service-utility (SaaS-U) concepts, which are emerging concepts for current and future networked enterprises.

SaaS is a model of software deployment where an application is hosted as a service provided to customers across the Internet. By eliminating the need to install and run the application on the customer's own computer, SaaS alleviates the customer's burden of software maintenance, ongoing operation, and support. Conversely, customers relinquish control over software versions or changing requirements.

Using SaaS also can conceivably reduce the up-front expense of software purchases, through less costly, on-demand pricing. From the software vendor's standpoint, SaaS has the attraction of providing stronger protection of its intellectual property and establishing an ongoing revenue stream. The SaaS software vendor may host the application on its own web server, or this function may be handled by a third-party application service provider (ASP). This way, end users may also reduce their investment on server hardware.

SaaS is generally associated with business software and is typically thought of as a low-cost way for businesses to obtain the same benefits of commercially licensed, internally operated software without the associated complexity and high initial cost. Many types of software are well suited to the SaaS model, where customers may have little interest or capability in software deployment, but do have substantial computing needs. Application areas such as Customer Relationship Management, video conferencing, human resources, IT service management, accounting, IT security, web analytics, web content management and e-mail are some of the initial markets showing SaaS success. The distinction between SaaS and earlier applications delivered over the Internet is that SaaS solutions were developed specifically to leverage web technologies such as the browser, thereby making them web-native. The data design and architecture of SaaS applications are specifically built with a 'multi-tenant' backend, thus enabling multiple customers or users to access a shared data model. This further differentiates SaaS from client/server or ASP solutions because SaaS providers are leveraging enormous economies of scale in the deployment, management, support and through the Software Development Lifecycle.

The ongoing European research is trying to make a new implementation of the SaaS vision, a step forward in a new field of interoperability among collaborative enterprises, supporting the various collaborative business forms, from supply chains to business ecosystems, and becoming for them like a utility, a commodity, the so-called Interoperability Service Utility (ISU).

The ISU challenge is addressed by COIN by providing a service infrastructure for Enterprise Interoperability in the business context of Enterprise Collaboration. This will not just create a service platform, but mainly a new business concept – the Software-as-a-Service Utility (SaaS-U) model.

The SaaS-U paradigm fits well with the ISU concepts and can be seen as a software application delivery model where a software vendor develops Web-native software services and hosts and operates them for use by its customers over the Internet. Customers do not pay for owning the software itself any longer but rather for using it on-demand. They use it through an API accessible over the Web and often written using Web services.

Furthermore, the SaaS-U paradigm also fits well with modern service-oriented architecture (SOA) that aim to promote software development in a way that leverages the construction of dynamic software systems and which can easily adapt to volatile user environments and be easily maintained as well. SOA enables flexible connectivity of applications by representing every application as a service with a standardized interface. This enables them to exchange structured information quickly and flexibly. This flexibility enables new and existing applications to be easily and quickly combined to address changing business needs, and the ability to easily combine and choreograph applications allows IT services to more readily reflect business processes.

In order to transform a generic (web) service into a utility it is mandatory to describe and understand what are the requirements that "make" a utility. The COIN consortium since now has identified the following requirements:

- **General Applicability.** To satisfy a generic, common need
- **Standards Based.** To adopt known and recognized international or domain standards.

- **Critical Mass of Providers.** To attract a certain number of service providers which could be interested in providing such a service.
- **Ubiquitous Access.** To be universally accessible.
- **Guaranteed SLAs (Service Level Agreement).** To be simultaneously accessible by anybody under guaranteed service levels.
- **Simple Configuration.** To require minimum configurations to be put in to action.
- **Simple Outcomes.** To be simply accessed by all and to provide clear and simple outcomes.
- **Simple Verification & Validation.** To allow easily testing, verification and simulation of the declared functionality.
- **Low cost.** To be available at low cost, under subscription or pay-per-use models.
- **Abundantly available.** To be available generally to all, with no rivalry.
- **Public Good.** To be a public good, not in the exclusive hands of single private entity.

## 5 Ongoing Activities and Preliminary Results

Interoperability between processes also implies the capability of the two processes to exchange messages. The two processes manage incoming and outgoing messages in their own formats, which can be incompatible, for instance, in terms of terminology, and data structuring. Harmonization of messages between the data organization of the sender and the receiver is needed. To this end, a semantics-based approach for business documents reconciliation (this task is part of the COIN sub-project "Information Interoperability services (IIS)") will support the semantic process interoperability. The semantic reconciliation assumes the existence (or the creation) of a shared ontology, among application that intend to communicate, as a common reference. The schema of the documents to be exchanged are mapped against the ontology (semantic annotation) in order to build transformation rules that allow the transformation of a document expressed in terms of the specific application format, to and from the ontology representation. Such rules are then applied when instances of document are actually exchanged. The activity of IIS starts from the semantic reconciliation suite developed in the ATHENA [3] and aim at enhancing it in order to provide an automatic support to the semantic mapping.

### 5.1 Tooling: Research, Candidates and Evaluation in Respect to SaaS

The CBPip process is a complex task that starts with a modelling activity and finish with an execution activity. Currently the COIN consortium is concentrating in the modelling phase. The choice of the tools to be used during this phase is critical if we want to enhance the SaaS and SaaS-U models.

The evaluation of the tools to be used in the modelling phase has to respect the following requirements:

- **Open source:** the chosen tools must be completely free and usable.
- **Standard based:** the tools must work with standard formats recognised by international bodies.

- **Completely web-based:** the users must not be required to install anything. Everything must be accessible from everywhere with a simple browser.

There are few candidates that respect all of the requirements specified above.

For the modelling tool the COIN consortium is evaluating the following tools:

- bxModeller [7]
- Oryx [8]
- ProcessMaker [9]

All the above mentioned tools are BPMN designers, which is the modeling language chosen for the CBPip process.

## 5.2   Transformation from Private Process to View Process

The aim of a transformation of a private process into a view process is to ease the specification of a public process which other companies can use and compose in a bigger setting; this public process will provide enough information and operations in order to call the private process, which will perform the real action.

The current version of the transformation, in MOFScript [10], implements a nearly complete privacy of the private process, meaning only the necessary operations remain during the transformation. COIN will study other means to lower such privacy, allowing for instance a partial view of the sub-processes that form the private process.

Figure 4 illustrates the transformation into a view process. This transformation works as follow:

- Copy each public operations from the View Process into the Public Process;
- Provide an operation in the View Process, which will perform the call to the Private Process
- Provide an operation in the View Process, which will be informed of the end of the Private Process

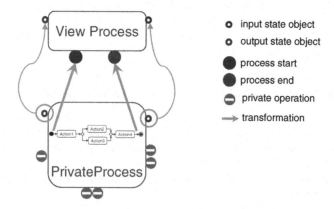

**Fig. 4.** Transformation of a private process into a view process

### 5.3  CBPip Post-execution Analysis with CBPip Modeling

With the means of CBPipM described in the previous section, the event log files of the IBM WebSphere Process Server [14] are roughly analyzed as a first step to the proof-of-concept. This section describes the preliminary identified pros and contras of CBPipM approach, where the lists are by no means complete (and proven) yet.

**PRO arguments:**
- "interoperability" as a model element associated with a formal specification and visualization which can be utilized for "post business process execution analysis (evidence search for a successfully executed CBP PSM)"
- The CBPip Framework described in the previous section can be extended in order to support the concepts of CBPipM
- CBPipM enables business process modeling and analysis on PSM and PIM levels, e.g. BPEL
- A new modeling technique to research on.
- Concentrates on basic interoperability issues: data, data semantic mapping and peek-to-peek transactions
- Provides model element unification, therefore applicability to both heterogeneous and homogeneous interoperability model transformation.
- Exposes multiple points to integrate appropriate semantic annotation and semantic mediation interoperability, human collaboration services.
- Aligned to UML2 modeling concepts, e.g. object flows.

**CONTRA arguments:**
- additional feasibility effort (proof of concept)
- CBPipM's consensus to business interoperability service architecture
- additional meta-modeling and model transformation effort

## 6  Conclusions and Future Work

The future work will concentrate on the three work packages, namely " BP modeling enhancement", "Transformation from Private Process to View Process", and "CBPip post-execution analysis", that are described in the following subordinated sections.

Furthermore, there are two topics that will gain momentum in the future: applying semantic annotation and usage of COIN semantic services, and integration of the deliverables of the work packages "Transformation into a View Process" and "CBPip post-execution analysis" as "BP modeling enhancements".

### 6.1  BP Modeling Enhancement: Next Steps

The COIN choice for the modelling tool is bxModeller [7] because among the different candidates proposed it is the one with the clearest architecture and uses the most known technologies.

The first step for the modelling enhancements is the customization of such modeller to allow the users to define private and public attributes on the activities and perform the call to the PP/VP transformation services.

## 6.2 Transformation into a View Process: Next Steps

The current version of the transformation allows only a high level of privacy of the processes, as it focuses only on public / private operations, providing a 'black box view' of the private process. We are currently investigating in ways to produce a more 'grey box view', where the View Process will show a partial control flow of the private process. This implies transformation rules for operations to monitor the state of the private process.

## 6.3 CBPip Post-execution Analysis: Next Steps

Regarding to CBPip post-execution analysis with CBPip Modeling, the work will continue on to specify the CBPipM concepts precisely and in detail, to define the CBPipM meta-model with a given modeling notation, e.g. BPMN, SoaML, and to define and describe transformation formalisms text-2-model, e.g. event log structure to UML transformation. Additionally, the verification of CBP execution by the means of CBPipM will be investigated.

# References

1. COIN, COIN Home Page, COIN IP, http://www.coin-ip.eu/ (last visited 2009)
2. ECOLEAD, ECOLEAD Home Page, http://ecolead.vtt.fi/ (last visited 2009)
3. ATHENA, ATHENA Home Page, ATHENA IP, http://www.athena-ip.org/ (last visited 2007)
4. SHAPE, SHAPE Home Page, http://www.shape-project.eu/ (last visited 2009)
5. MDA, Model Driven Architecture, Object Management Group (OMG), http://www.omg.org/mda/ (last visited 2009)
6. BPMN, Business Process Modeling Notation, http://www.omg.org/bpmn/ (last visited 2009)
7. bxModeller, an open source web-based application tool for business process modeling, http://semantics.eng.it/bxmodeller/http://semantics.eng.it/bxmodeller/ (last visited 2009)
8. Oryx, an open source web-based application tool for business process modeling, http://bpt.hpi.uni-potsdam.de/Oryx/BPMN (last visited 2009)
9. ProcessMaker, an open source web-based application tool for business process management and workflow modeling, http://www.processmaker.com/ (last visited 2009)
10. Oldevik, J., Neple, T., Grønmo, R., Aagedal, J., Berre, A.: Toward Standardised Model to Text Transformations. In: European Conference on Model Driven Architecture - Foundations and Applications (ECMDA), Nuremberg (November 2005)
11. SoaML, Service oriented architecture Modeling Language, http://www.omg.org/docs/ad/08-08-04.pdf (last visited 2009)
12. BPEL, Web Services Business Process Execution Language, http://www.oasis-open.org/specs/#wsbpelv2.0 (last visited 2009)
13. Elvesæter, B., Del Grosso, E., Capellini, A., Taglino, F., Benguria, G.: Towards Enterprise Interoperability Service Utilities. In: IWEI 2008 workshop (2008)
14. IBM WebSphere, a business process execution engine, http://www-01.ibm.com/software/integration/wps/ (last visited 2009)

# Barriers to Enterprise Interoperability

Johan Ullberg[1], David Chen[2], and Pontus Johnson[1]

[1] Industrial Information and Control Systems, KTH - Royal Institute of Technology,
10044, Stockholm, Sweden
{johanu,pj101}@ics.kth.se
[2] IMS/LAPS, University Bordeaux 1,
351, Cours de la liberation, 33405 Talence cedex, France
david.chen@ims-bordeaux.fr

**Abstract.** Interoperability is a key feature for enterprises in today's competitive environment. Fundamental interoperability problems are however still not well understood. Within the scope of the Framework for Enterprise Interoperability (FEI) originally proposed by INTEROP NoE and now moved to ISO standardization process, this paper tentatively identifies and categorizes a set of interoperability barriers. Barriers to interoperability are defined as incompatibility between two enterprise systems. A list of interoperability barriers is presented and these barriers are then mapped to the FEI and illustrated with examples. The most significant dependencies between barriers are also tentatively defined and presented.

**Keywords:** Framework for Enterprise Interoperability, interoperability barrier, interoperability concern, interoperability dependency.

## 1 Introduction

Interoperability development has been approached from many different points of view and perspectives, such as computer science, collaboration in the frame of networked enterprise, etc. However fundamental interoperability problems are still not well understood and they are only fragmentally considered and studied. This paper proposes to identify interoperability problems through the concept of barrier and to tackle interoperability development by a problem driven approach. The research assumptions are as follows:

1. Enterprises are not interoperable because there are barriers to interoperability that obstruct exchange of information and services.
2. Barriers are incompatibilities of various kinds and can be found at various levels and domains of an enterprise.
3. Incompatibilities have as source the heterogeneity between the actors that are to interoperate. Whenever there is heterogeneity in two related systems, there is a risk of interoperability problems.
4. Barriers can be specific linked to a specific application; however there exist generic barriers which are common in all situations of non interoperability.

R. Poler, M. van Sinderen, and R. Sanchis (Eds.): IWEI 2009, LNBIP 38, pp. 13–24, 2009.

Based on the assumptions made, the research in Enterprise Interoperability domain consists in elaborating solutions to remove barriers (i.e. incompatibilities between systems or components of systems that are concerned by interoperations).

The objective of this paper is to contribute to a better understanding of interoperability problems by identifying and structuring barriers to interoperability under the guidance of an interoperability framework.

Recently several initiatives on interoperability have proposed interoperability frameworks to structure issues and concerns in quite different ways. The European Interoperability Framework in the eGovernment domain [1] defines three types of interoperability: semantic, technical and organizational. A similar approach was also proposed in e-Health interoperability framework [2] which identified three layers: organizational, informational and technical interpretabilities. In manufacturing area the IDEAS interoperability framework [3] defines three main layers (Business, Knowledge and ICT) with two additional vertical dimensions (Semantics and Quality attributes). More recently the ATHENA Interoperability Framework (AIF) proposes to structure interoperability issues and solutions at the three levels: conceptual, technical and applicative [4].

This paper adopts the Framework for Enterprise Interoperability [5] which was initially proposed within the INTEROP DI and now under the process of standardization (CEN/ISO 11354). This framework covers the main issues identified in the previously mentioned frameworks and focuses on the problem dimension of interoperability. The objective is to tackle interoperability problems through the identification of barriers which prevent interoperability to occur.

The remainder of this paper is structured as follows: The introduction to the field of interoperability in this section is in the next section followed by a brief introduction to the Framework for Enterprise Interoperability. In section 3 the main contribution of the paper is presented, a set of barriers and their mapping into the framework. The internal relationships between these barriers are then elaborated in section 4 followed by a conclusion of the paper in section 5.

## 2   The Framework for Enterprise Interoperability

The Framework for Enterprise Interoperability defines the three basic dimensions as follows:

- *Interoperability concerns* which defines the content of interoperation that may take place at various levels of the enterprise (data, service, process, business) i.e. the level at which the interoperation occurs.
- *Interoperability barriers* which identifies various obstacles to interoperability in three categories (conceptual, technological, and organizational), i.e. the type of obstacle to interoperability.
- *Interoperability approaches* which represents the different ways in which barriers can be removed (integrated, unified, and federated).

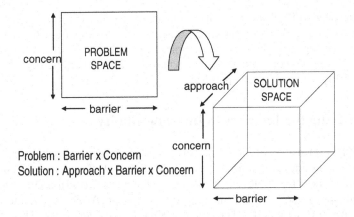

**Fig. 1.** The relation between the problem and solution space of the framework

The first two dimensions: Interoperability concerns and Interoperability barriers constitute the problem space of enterprise interoperability, see Fig. 1. The intersection of an interoperability barrier and an interoperability concern is the set of interoperability problems having the same barrier and concern. The three dimensions together constitute the solution space of enterprise interoperability. The intersection of an interoperability barrier, an interoperability concern and an interoperability approach is the set of solutions to overcome an interoperability barrier at a level of concern, using a specific approach.

Three categories of barriers are defined: conceptual barriers (syntactic and semantic incompatibilities), technological barriers (additional incompatibility due to the use of technology), and organizational barriers (related to the incompatibilities of method of work, organization structure, etc.). These barriers can exist at four different levels of concerns: data, service, process and business levels. Fig. 2 shows the interoperability framework in its simplified form with only the first two dimensions defining the problem space.

| Iop concerns \ Iop barriers | CONCEPTUAL | TECHNOLOGICAL | ORGANISATIONAL |
|---|---|---|---|
| BUSINESS | | | |
| PROCESS | | | |
| SERVICE | | | |
| DATA | | | |

**Fig. 2.** Interoperability Framework (here only the first two dimensions)

The interoperability framework also aims at structuring interoperability solutions according to their ability to remove the barriers. This is important for retrieval and reuses the existing knowledge. For example, PSL (Process Specification Language) allows removing the conceptual barrier (syntactic and semantic barriers) for process interoperability using a unified approach.

# 3   Identifying the Barriers to Interoperability

Although the dimensions of the framework are well defined, see section 2, the actual barriers and solutions are still not yet explicitly identified. This paper sets out to detail the barriers at the different levels of concerns, give a brief description of each barrier and provide an example of how this barrier could occur. An ID is given to each barrier allowing to categorize the barriers according to the framework. This ID is constructed according to the following syntax: <type of barrier>'/'<type of concern>'-'< number within this category>, where the types are identified by the first letter in their respective names. For instance, O/P-2 is the second organizational barrier at the process level. The description of barrier is expressed as the heterogeneity (or difference of things) considered as the source of incompatibilities (barriers).

**Table 1.** List of the barriers with ID, name and a brief description

| Id | Name | Description |
|---|---|---|
| C/D-1 | Data content | Coverage, i.e. content, of the respective data representation |
| C/D-2 | Data syntax | Heterogeneous data format and structure |
| C/D-3 | Data semantics | Data meaning disagreements |
| C/S-1 | Service content | Differences in the coverage, i.e. content, of the services offered |
| C/S-2 | Service syntax | Language/formalism syntax used to describe the services |
| C/S-3 | Service semantics | The meaning of services descriptions |
| C/P-1 | Process content | Coverage, i.e. content, of the processes |
| C/P-2 | Process syntax | Process description language grammar and graphical representation |
| C/P-3 | Process semantics | The meaning of the processes description |
| C/B-1 | Visions, strategies & Culture | Differences in the respective companies goals, views, etc. |
| C/B-2 | Business syntax | Format, template or model used for describing enterprise business |
| C/B-3 | Business semantics | Meaning of terms used to express business issues |
| T/D-1 | Exchange format | Protocol or format available to exchange information |
| T/S-1 | Service granularity | Definitions of what constitutes the services, i.e. interface problems |

**Table 1.** (*continued*)

| T/P-1 | Process behavior | Order of operations in the computerized processes |
|---|---|---|
| T/B-1 | Degree of computerization | How much of data, services and processes that are automated in IT |
| T/B-2 | IT requirement fulfillment | The ability of IT to support the requirements of the business |
| O/D-1 | Information ownership | The structures for assigning rights to data |
| O/D-2 | Classified information | Differences in which information that is to be regarded as classified with respect to the collaboration partner |
| O/S-1 | Resource control | The allocation of resources, technical as well as non technical. |
| O/P-1 | Business process behavior | Order of operation in business processes |
| O/B-1 | Legislation | The legislative requirements that influence different actors. |
| O/B-2 | Organization structure | How enterprises are organized on a high level |
| O/B-3 | Methods of work | High level differences regarding how work is performed in the organizations |

The remainder of this chapter provides explanation and examples of barriers listed above. The examples are elaborated within the context of two retail organizations E1 and E2 that want to interoperate in order to cover a larger market both in terms of geographical coverage and type of merchandise.

## 3.1 Conceptual Barriers

The conceptual barriers are mainly concerned with the syntactic and semantic incompatibilities of information to be exchanged. These problems concern the modeling at the high level of abstraction as well as the information level [6]. Generally speaking the conceptual barriers can be classified into three different types, see Fig. 3.

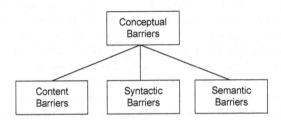

**Fig. 3.** The three main types of conceptual barriers: content, syntactic and semantic barriers

**Table 2.** Different types of semantic conflicts, (1) same term with different definitions and (2) different terms with the same definition, adopted from [7]

|          | T1=T2              | T1≠T2            |
|----------|--------------------|------------------|
| D1=D2    | Conflict of type 1 | No conflict      |
| D1≠D2    | No conflict        | Conflict of type 2 |

The content barrier is related to the coverage of the models within the enterprises, and heterogeneity would correspond to some concepts of one of the companies that do not exist in the other company. Syntactic barriers are concerned with the language used to express models and the semantic barriers with the meaning of the terms used.

On the data level the C/D-1 relates to difference in the content of data stored by the enterprises. For example, E1 uses the social security number for identification of their customers whereas E2 uses a customer ID and thus does not have social security number stored regarding their customers.

E1 also encode their customers' names using just a "name" field containing the concatenation of the given name and surname. E2 on the other hand uses two fields, one "name" field containing the given name and one "surname" field containing the surname. This corresponds to the barrier C/D-2 (data syntax barrier).

Turning to the data semantic barrier (C/D-3), with the assumption that a concept C=(T,D) consists of a term, T and a definition D, two cases of barriers are identified, cf. Table 2: (1) the same term is used with different meanings (definitions), (2) the same concept (equal definitions) is named with different terms. This view is an aggregation of the six semantic problems as outlined in [7].

Data semantic barrier is the most frequently encountered interoperability problem. For example, the enterprises E1 and E2 both use the term "Shipped" to refer to items that are sold and will be delivered to the customer. E1 however, use this term to refer only to the items actually in transit, i.e. items that have left the premises of E1 and are on their way to the customer. E2 have a wider meaning and regard an item to be shipped as soon as it's sold, regardless if the actual shipping has commenced. E1 and E2 also use the terms "invoice" and "receipt" respectively to refer to the same item, i.e. the customers' proof of purchase.

At the service level, the same problem of content, syntax and semantics occur. The content barrier (C/S-1) occurs if for example E1 defines the service "pay by check" but E2 doesn't accept payment through checks. Regarding the syntax of services (C/S-2), the choice of language to describe the services is an important question, E1 use a more formal language that stipulates that the specification of a service as structured information, using fields like "name", "input", "output", "operations". E2 on the other hand use unstructured descriptions of their services, with just paragraphs of text describing the same information as contained in E1s descriptions.

Just as in the case of data, the semantics of the services (C/S-3) is concerned with the meaning of terms used for different services, one example could be that E1 and E2 both use the service "register monetary payment" but E1 refers to any form of direct payment whereas E2 only to payment by cash.

At the process level, different process content (C/P-1) may lead to incompatible process collaboration. For example E2 does not work with installments and thus does not have a process for evaluating a customer's credit rating and updating these ratings, something done in E1 where installments are a frequent means of payment. The syntax barrier (C/P-2) is mainly concerned with the use of different process modeling languages (for example, UML and BPMN). This syntax barrier is the main problem in exchanging process models between companies and to relate them together to build collaborative processes. Finally the semantic barrier at process level (C/P-3) refers to the meaning of the terms used to name and describe processes and sub-processes. For example E1 uses the term "procurement" to refer to exactly the same process as E2 have named "acquisitions" and that the process "claims management" exists in both E1 and E2 and deals with return of faulty goods, however the individual steps in this process are different in the respective companies.

Regarding conceptual barriers at the business level, C/B-1 (different strategy and vision) exists if one company adopts a Low cost strategy consisting in selling the product by lowering costs and maximizing income (by increasing volume), while another company focuses on aiding the customer to increase the added value in the customers organization. Differentiation in this way usually includes the act of getting involved in your customer's processes [8].

Even if C/B-1 corresponds to the content issue of the conceptual barriers, there is still however the matter of communicating this content between the enterprises, if different languages are used to encode vision, goals. For example if one uses natural language in policy documents whereas the other one uses the modeling notation Business motivation model [9], this will lead to the C/B-2 syntactic barrier. The semantic problem (C/B-3) also occurs at business level. For example E1 and E2 use the term "leading" differently in statements such as "We will be the leading supplier of industrial tools on the US market". E1 interprets 'leading' as the supplier with the largest turnover whereas E2 interprets it as having the most advanced tools on the market.

## 3.2 Technological Barriers

The technological barriers are concerned with the use of computer or ICT (Information and Communication Technology) to communicate and exchange information [6].

Barriers in the technological domain at the data level (T/D-1) are encountered when it is impossible to exchange data files or access to the database of a third system. This may occur when two systems don't share an exchange format, for example the ERP system of E1 has the options of using an internal proprietary data format or a XML based industry standard. E2 on the other hand is only able to exchange information in an EDI based format such as UN/EDIFACT. Moreover since different versions of the same exchange format might be incompatible it's important to specify the exchange format in a manner so that the compatibility is ensured (i.e. including version number etc.). This barrier could be further broken down into the different types of conceptual barriers described above, see C/D-1, 2 and 3.

Enterprises may also define their services with different degrees of granularity leading to an interoperability barrier (T/S-1). For example E1 might have an order system with the services "add item" (corresponding to adding a row on the order) and "update stock" (which corresponds to reducing the number shown as available in stock). E2 could have defined their services to one single "register row" which performs both operations. Even though the actual actions might be exactly the same, i.e. adding an item to the order always follows by a reduction in stock and there are no conceptual differences between the systems, there will still be a barrier in terms of the defined interfaces of the respective systems.

Within the technological domain at the process level the barrier process behavior is concerned with incompatibilities of process execution tools to work together. The barrier, T/P-1, is not specifically coupled with the use of paradigms such as SOA/Workflows although the name might indicate so – the order in which operations are performed in systems have always been of high importance. This barrier is very similar to the O/P-1 barrier in the organizational domain. In E1 the process of registering a sale, and thus the operations of the system that supports this task, is to first take the customer information and then to register the items whereas E2 might have defined the same process in the opposite order, i.e. register the items first and then taking the customers details.

At the business level, barrier T/B-1 refers to differences in degree of computerization. One company may for example have decided and implemented a fully computerized invoice process so that once an order is sent the invoice is sent as well. Another company on the other hand chooses a manual process where each order is audited by personnel that then manually enter the invoices in the billing system. This is essentially a difference in the requirements posed on IT.

Related to the matter of requirement is the barrier T/B-2 that is concerned with how well IT actually supports the requirements of the organization. Even if the requirements of the business on IT are matched between the interoperating organizations it's not necessary the case that the ability of the respective IT organizations to fulfill these requirements are equal. This will primarily become a barrier to interoperability as the cooperation between the enterprises unfold, typically problems relating to a joint decision to change the cooperation in some manner and this affects IT. If the enterprises decide to create a joint shop, for instance on the web, this will pose new requirements on IT and a discrepancy in the ability to fulfill these requirements will become a barrier. This can be seen as a somewhat coarse black box view of this fairly complex issue of matching IT and business, and is also somewhat related to the concept of B-ITa, see for instance [10] for more information about B-ITa in collaborative networked organizations.

## 3.3 Organizational Barriers

The organizational barriers are concerned with the incompatibilities of organization structure and management techniques implemented in two enterprises [6]. Generally speaking, different ways of defining and assigning responsibility and authority result in different organizations which may raise problems from the interoperability point of view. At the data level different structures for data or information ownership (O/D-1) is an organizational barrier. For example if E1 only allows changes in customer information to be performed by customer support whereas E2 allows the same changes from both customer support and sales. Generally there are four different access rights for data, these are Create, Modify, Access and Remove, in the above example Customer support of E1 assigned C, M & R to customer support and A to both customer support and sales. In E2 on the other hand both customer support and sales were assigned the whole set of C, M, A & R. Another problem relating to the data level is differences in the amount of information each partner is willing to share, O/D-2.

E1 could benefit greatly from information on previous sales in order to improve the joint marketing but E2 have a policy stating that such information must not leave the company.

Regarding the service level, O/S-1, E1 have an organizational policy where, in the case of workforce resources, the resources themselves determine if they are available to perform a task and usage of IT resources are decided by the IT department. E2 on the other hand have a policy where the head of each department is responsible for allocating the time of the employees and the IT resources are owned by the business rather than the IT department and the resources are thus allocated by the head of the business department.

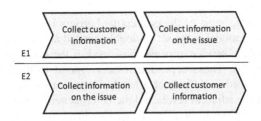

**Fig. 4.** An example of incompatibility in the order of business process execution, O/P-1

The organizational barrier at the process level, O/P-1, is concerned with the behavioral aspects of the processes in the enterprises. In E1s customer service department all information about the customer is collected before information about the customer's problem is attained, the order of the same process in E2 use the opposite order, see Fig. 4.

E1, being listed on NASDAQ need to be compliant with the Sarbanes-Oxley Act while E2 that is listed on the Swedish stock exchange and by that is required to comply with the Swedish Code of Corporate Governance. These two codes of conduct are somewhat heterogeneous thus leading to a legislative barrier, O/B-1.

The organizational structures of the enterprise, O/B-2, is also of importance to the ability to interoperate, if one enterprise is organized in terms of a functional organization with for instance a head of the sales department whereas the other defines a matrix organization where the employees working with sales have two managers. For the respective managers to find their counterpart in the other organization could be difficult. Differences in organizational structure will most likely also lead to differences in methods of work which is the next and final barrier, O/B-3. One example of this barrier is when one company require that working hours shall be seven hours a day and forty hours a week (five hours on Saturday), whereas the other company stipulates eight hours a day and forty-four hours a week (four hours to be dealt at anytime at the workplace) [8].

## 4   Relationships between the Barriers

Many of the barriers described in section 3 are in some way related to each other. The most obvious relationship is those defined by the categorization of barriers in the two dimensions "barriers" and "concerns", e.g. all conceptual barriers are related and all process level barriers are related. This section will elaborate on how barriers are affected by other barriers rather than covering these basic relationships, as long as the basic relationships don't coincide with dependencies. The dependencies will be presented in models, the corresponding metamodel is very simple, with just one entity, the barrier, and one relationship, the affect relationship illustrated by an arrow indicating that the source barrier affects the target barrier.

For readability reasons the barriers and their relationships have been divided into two clusters, the first contains primarily conceptual barriers and the second primarily the organizational and technical barriers. Between these two clusters only one relationship exists and in order to cover this relationship the barrier business process behavior exists in both models.

The model containing most of the conceptual barriers is shown in Fig. 6. Perhaps most noticeable in this model is the set of double headed arrows between the different levels of concerns (data, service, process, business) of the same type of barrier (content, syntax, semantics). These dependencies correspond to the idea that what has been conceptually agreed or defined at a level of concern would affect what will be agreed or defined at the adjacent levels and the heterogeneities would follow the same pattern. For each given situation only one of the directions exist, which one is dependent on whether the enterprises define their content, syntax and semantics bottom-up (i.e. starting at the data level and working their way up) or top-down.

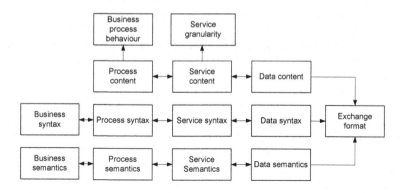

**Fig. 5.** First part of dependency structure mainly covering the conceptual barriers

Barriers at the data models content, syntax and semantics would also affect the exchange format since the data being exchange is based on the data model. Differences in the process content could influence the behavior of the business processes and service content heterogeneities often lead to interface problems, as described by the service granularity barrier.

Turning to the rest of the barriers and their relationships, cf. Fig. 7, recall that the barrier business process behavior is the link from the previous model. In this model one double headed arrow exists as well, linking business process behavior to system behavior. Just as before only one of the directions is valid for each case corresponding to whether the enterprise have a policy of altering the systems to conform to the business or if the business adopts the behavior of the system. Barriers at the business process behavior could depend on differences in the high level methods of work. The methods of work in turn can mainly be affected by barriers relating to organization structure, vision, strategy and culture as well as legislative differences.

The vision, strategy and culture barrier could be claimed to, at least indirectly, influence most of the other barriers, however the most direct affect is that on organization structure, classified information and finally IT requirements fulfillment. The last B-ITa related barrier in turn affects the degree of computerization. Since the organization structure often defines responsibilities within the organization both the information ownership and resource control barriers are affected by the organization structure barrier. Furthermore, controlling resources often lead to controlling information as well and thus there is a dependency between these barriers. Finally the information classification barrier could, apart from what was described before, also be affected by legislative differences and differences in information ownership.

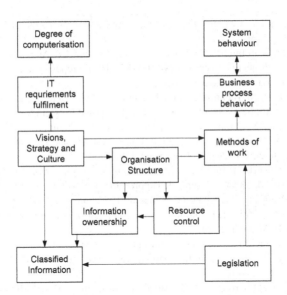

**Fig. 6.** Dependencies between barriers primarily from the organizational and technical domain

## 5  Conclusion

This paper set out to identify the set of interoperability barriers that obstruct the interoperation between enterprise systems. The list presented is not exhaustive and needs to be further completed and refined. Incompatibility resulting from heterogeneity of system elements is considered as a key concept to identify barriers and to understand various problems of interoperability. Solutions to improve interoperability are under constant development, but it's not until the problem space is exhaustively identified and clearly defined that it's possible to assure that the available solutions really mitigate all the barriers. Well defined problems (i.e. the barriers) can also aid in efficient development of solutions to these problems.

The conceptual barriers are the most important ones because they are concerned with the presentation and representation of concepts to use for enterprise business and operations. Technological barriers are additional barriers stemming from existing incompatible information technologies. Organizational barriers are also additional barriers due to particularly incompatible human behaviors. The barriers are not independent and the most important dependencies between barriers are also shown in the paper.

Future work is to validate the proposed list of barriers through case studies and elaborate an interoperability maturity model based on the concepts of barriers identified.

# References

1. EIF: European Interoperability Framework, White Paper, Brussels, 18 (Feburary 2004), http://www.comptia.org
2. NEHTA: Towards an Interoperability Framework, Version 1.8, August 21 (2005)
3. IDEAS: IDEAS Project Deliverables (WP1-WP7), Public reports (2003), http://www.ideas-roadmap.net
4. ATHENA: Advanced Technologies for Interoperability of Heterogeneous Enterprise Networks and their Applications, FP6-2002-IST-1, Integrated Project (April 2003)
5. Chen, D., Daclin, N.: Framework for Enterprise Interoperability. In: EI2N 2nd International Workshop on Enterprise Integration, Interoperability and Networking, in Second International Conference I-ESA 2006, France (2006)
6. Chen, D.: Framework for Enterprise Interoperability. In: 8th Congrès International de Génie Industriel (CIGI 2009), Bagnères de Bigorre, France (2009)
7. Zouggar, N., Vallespir, B., Chen, D.: Semantic Enrichment of Enterprise Models by Ontologies-based Semantic Annotations. In: International Workshop on Enterprise Interoperability (IWEI), Munich (2009)
8. Guedria, W., Naudet, Y., Chen, D.: Contribution of System Theory to develop Enterprise Interoperability. In: 8th Congrès International de Génie Industriel (CIGI 2009), Bagnères de Bigorre, France (2009)
9. Object Management Group (OMG), Business Motivation Model (BMM) Specification (August 2008), http://www.omg.org/spec/BMM/1.0/
10. Santana Tapia, R., Daneva, M., van Eck, P., Wieringa, R.: Towards a Business-IT Alignment Maturity Model for Collaborative Networked Organizations. In: International Workshop on Enterprise Interoperability (IWEI), Munich (2009)

# A SOA-Based Platform-Specific Framework for Context-Aware Mobile Applications*

Laura M. Daniele, Eduardo Silva, Luís Ferreira Pires, and Marten van Sinderen

Centre for Telematics and Information Technology,
University of Twente, Enschede, The Netherlands
{l.m.daniele,e.m.g.silva,l.ferreirapires,
m.j.vansinderen}@ewi.utwente.nl

**Abstract.** Context-aware mobile applications are intelligent applications that can monitor the user's context and, in case of changes in this context, consequently adapt their behaviour in order to satisfy the user's current needs or anticipate the user's intentions. The design of such applications relies on dynamic middleware platforms that consist of a variety of components. These components are distributed in the environment and interoperate by making use of each other's services. In the A-MUSE project, we defined a design methodology based on MDA principles that relies on a SOA reference architecture for context-aware mobile applications. This paper shows how abstract concepts in the design of such applications can be applied to realize concrete components that guarantee architectural interoperability. We also present a platform-specific framework that uses BPEL, UDDI registry and web services as target technologies to implement our reference architecture.

**Keywords:** Service-Oriented Architecture, Model-Driven Architecture, context-awareness, BPEL, web services, UDDI.

## 1 Introduction

Context-aware mobile applications are intelligent applications that can monitor the user's context and, in case of changes in this context, consequently adapt their behaviour in order to satisfy the user's current needs or anticipate the user's intentions. For example, a context-aware mobile phone could be able to know when its user is sitting in a movie theatre and consequently mutes itself without explicit user's intervention. When the user is travelling and dinner time is approaching, the same context-aware mobile phone could suggest a suitable restaurant based on the user's location and his/her previous dining history. Anywhere and anytime, context-aware mobile applications should be able to provide relevant services to their users. The design of such applications relies on dynamic middleware platforms that consist of a variety of components [1,8,11,12]. These components are distributed in the environment and interoperate by making use of each other's services.

---

* This work is part of the Freeband A-MUSE Project (http://a-muse.freeband.nl). Freeband is sponsored by the Dutch government under contract BSIK 03025.

R. Poler, M. van Sinderen, and R. Sanchis (Eds.): IWEI 2009, LNBIP 38, pp. 25–37, 2009.

In the A-MUSE project, we have defined a middleware platform based on a reference architecture tailored to context-aware mobile applications. This reference architecture includes all the components typically used by such applications. In [4] we have also defined an (automated) design approach based on this reference architecture. This approach refines the monolithic abstract specification of a context-aware mobile application into the distributed behaviour of concrete components that interoperate with each other in order to achieve the goals of the application. This paper aims at showing how the abstract concepts in the design can be mapped to concrete components that guarantee interoperability in our reference architecture, and how these components can be built with specific target technologies. Towards this aim, we have defined and implemented a framework based on specific target technologies that is correct and consistent with the original monolithic abstract specification of our applications. We have made a specific choice on these target technologies, namely, we have used BPEL, UDDI registry and web services. However, our design is platform-independent and can be realized with other specific target implementations.

The structure of the paper is the following: Section 2 introduces the design methodology and reference architecture we have defined in the A-MUSE project for the development of context-aware mobile applications, Section 3 investigates which concrete architectural components are necessary to provide interoperability in the reference architecture and how these components can be built and integrated in a platform-specific framework, Section 4 presents a case study that illustrates how the abstract concepts of our reference architecture can be realized with the concrete components of the platform-specific framework, Section 5 discusses some related work, and Section 6 presents our conclusions and identifies topics for future work.

## 2   Design Methodology

This section introduces our reference architecture and the design methodology in which this architecture is embedded. The reference architecture has been defined and applied in the A-MUSE project to realize the Live Contacts case study [13,20]. Live Contacts consists of a context-aware mobile application that runs on Pocket PC phones, Smartphones and desktop PCs and allows its users to contact the right person, at the right time, at the right place, via the right communication channel. The reference architecture is general enough to be reused for other context-aware mobile applications by simply redefining some application-specific components, such as context sources and action providers. Moreover, the use of this architecture does not limit our design methodology to context-aware mobile applications, since the same methodology can be applied (with minor adjustments) to other categories of applications based on different reference architectures.

### 2.1   Reference Architecture

The control component of our reference architecture is the service coordinator, which receives events and triggers actions as reactions to these events. Events may be either *user input events*, which consist of explicit user requests to the application, or *context events*, which consist of relevant changes in the user context. For example, a user input event may be a request for the user's list of buddies, and a context event may be the proximity event triggered whenever a buddy is nearby the user. Actions represent application reactions to user input and context events, and may be an invocation of any internal or external service, such as the generation of a signal, the delivery of a notification or a web service request.

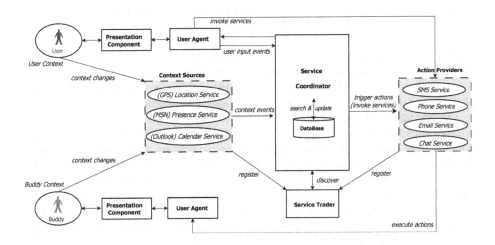

**Fig. 1.** A-MUSE reference architecture for context-aware mobile applications

Fig. 1 shows a single user instance that interacts with the system and a buddy of this user. The presentation component takes care of the interactions with the end-user and there is one presentation component for each user. In this paper, we do not provide any implementation of this component. The user agent (one for each user and located in the user device) interacts on behalf of the user with the presentation component to obtain user input and present user output, and provides the service coordinator with user input events. The service coordinator orchestrates all the other components, searching and updating a database, which contains information about users (e.g., name, password, preferred contact means and list of buddies). To simplify the discussion without loss of generality, we assume a system configuration with one service coordinator and one database. The service coordinator also interacts with context sources and action providers.

Context sources sense changes in the user context and provides the service coordinator with context events. Fig. 1 shows a (GPS) location service that provides information about users' current location, a (MSN) presence service that provides indications whether users registered in the application are available online in the network, and a (Outlook) calendar service that provides information about users' appointments and activities. We assume that there is one (GPS) location service, one (MSN) presence service and one (Outlook) calendar service for each user agent in this particular configuration. These services are registered in the service trader.

The action providers are responsible for performing actions that follow user input and context events. Fig. 1 shows an SMS service, phone service, e-mail service and chat service, which enable users to communicate with each other through sending messages, making a phone call, sending e-mails or chatting, respectively. These services are also registered in the service trader.

The service trader registers all the available services offered by context sources and action providers. This allows the coordinator to dynamically discover available services based on the service descriptions that are published in the service trader. After discovering the proper service, the coordinator can invoke it by using the endpoint location contained in the service description. Alternatively, the coordinator can forward this endpoint to the user agent, which can directly invoke the service without intervention of the coordinator. This use of a service trader is a well established pattern of service discovery in service-oriented architectures. Examples of service traders in middleware platforms are the OMG CORBA trader [17] and the UDDI registry [15].

The interactions among components of this architecture are based on the service-oriented architecture (SOA) approach, which considers components only from the point of view of the service that they provide or use without considering the internal details of how the service itself is implemented. According to SOA, components make use of each other's services to interoperate in order to support the goals of the application. In this paper, we focus on the right part of Fig. 1, namely on the interactions between the user agent, the coordinator, the database, the service trader and the action providers. Information on the interactions between the coordinator and context sources can be found in [3].

## 2.2   MDA-Based Methodology

The reference architecture of Fig. 1 has been defined as part of a design methodology based on the Model-Driven Architecture (MDA) approach [16]. Fig. 2 shows this methodology, which divides the design of context-aware mobile applications in different levels of models with different degrees of abstraction and platform-independence. The *service* specification is the highest level of abstraction and describes a context-aware mobile service[1] as a monolithic behaviour from an external perspective. At this level, we specify the functionality that our service offers to its user and we do not consider any structural detail of the service, i.e., we abstract from its internal components. The *platform-independent service design* model describes a context-aware mobile application from an internal perspective revealing our SOA-based reference architecture. The *platform-specific service design* model describes the realization of a context-aware mobile application in terms of specific target technologies. Several alternative Platform-Specific Models (PSMs) may implement a Platform-Independent Model (PIM) as long as correctness and consistency are guaranteed. Therefore, it is in principle possible to use different middleware technologies to realize the platform-specific service design.

---

[1] The term *service* at this level denotes the observable behaviour of the whole application, as opposed to the use of the term service in service-oriented architectures to denote the functionality supported by a service provider reachable from some middleware.

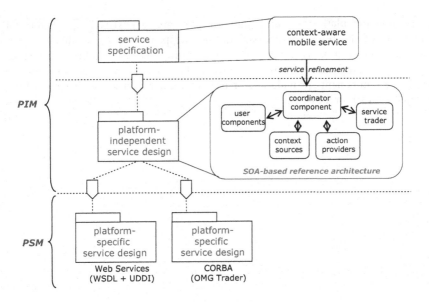

**Fig. 2.** MDA-based methodology

Our previous work [4,5] focuses on the PIM level of this methodology, namely on the service specification and platform-independent service design model, and the transformations between these models. These transformations consist of gradual (automated) refinements that preserve correctness and consistency particularly of behavioural aspects, which are usually overlooked at the PIM level in the MDA community [14]. This paper focuses on the transformation from the platform-independent to the platform-specific design models and provides an implementation framework for a specific part of the reference architecture, i.e., user agent, coordinator, database, service trader, and action providers. This implementation shows that the PSM level preserves the interoperability that we have designed at the PIM level.

## 3 Platform-Specific Framework

We consider the following scenario:

*"A user wants to contact one of his/her buddies with a specific communication means, such as SMS, phone, chat or e-mail. Therefore, the user provides the application with the name of this buddy and the communication means to be used. In order to fulfil the user request, the coordinator has to retrieve the contact details of the buddy from the buddy list of the user in the database, and discover a proper service in the service trader according to the desired communication means. Once the coordinator has retrieved contact details of the buddy and the endpoint location of the communication service, it can forward this information to the user agent, which is finally able to invoke the proper service and put the user in communication with the desired buddy".*

Fig. 3 shows our platform-specific framework for this scenario. In this framework, components of the reference architecture are mapped on target technologies. The same framework can be used with different scenarios. We realized the coordinator as BPEL process exposed as a web service to all the other components of the architecture. These components provide and/or use services, which are orchestrated by the coordinator BPEL process.

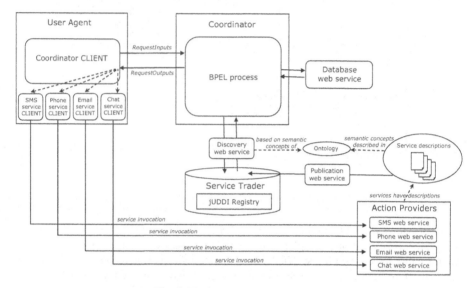

**Fig. 3.** Platform-specific framework

Fig. 3 shows that the coordinator BPEL process receives some inputs from the *coordinator client* in the user agent (*RequestInputs*). These inputs instantiate a new BPEL process. In the above mentioned scenario, the inputs are the name of the buddy and the preferred communication means to contact this buddy. In order to put the user in contact with his/her buddy, the coordinator BPEL process has to retrieve information from the database component, which is exposed in the framework as a web service (*database web service*). The coordinator BPEL process also needs to discover a suitable service in the *Service Trader* to provide the communication means selected by the user.

We realized the service trader as a UDDI registry using jUDDI [10], which is a Java implementation of the UDDI standard. Our jUDDI registry contains the descriptions of the services available in the framework. In our scenario, the available services are SMS, phone, e-mail and chat services. The service descriptions consist of XML documents with the name, type and endpoint of the service. The service type refers to semantic concepts described in an ontology supported by our framework. The endpoint is the concrete address where the service is deployed. Fig. 4 shows an example of service description for the SMS service. To support the publication of service descriptions in this format, we have extended the jUDDI with tModels that represent each of the service parameters, i.e., name, type and endpoint. To group the name, type and endpoint tModels under the same service, we have used the categoryBag UDDI element.

```
<ServiceDescription>
  <Name>SMS</Name>
  <Type>http://localhost:8080/ontologies/LiveContacts.owl#SmsService</Type>
  <Endpoint>http://localhost:8080/sms/services/sms</Endpoint>
</ServiceDescription>
```

**Fig. 4.** SMS service description

Service descriptions are published in our jUDDI registry through the *publication web service* in Fig. 3, which offers a publication interface to the service developers. This interface accepts a service description, parses this description and publishes the service name, type and endpoint in the jUDDI registry.

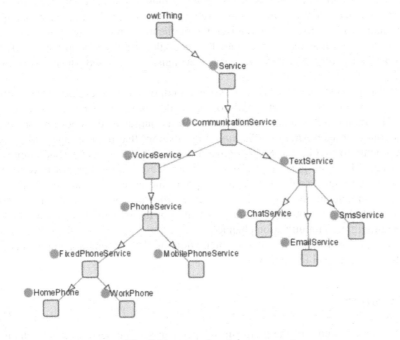

**Fig. 5.** Framework ontology excerpt

The coordinator BPEL process can discover the services published in the jUDDI registry through the *discovery web service* in Fig. 3. The discovery is based on the service type semantic concept, as the one used in the service descriptions. The discovery mechanism retrieves all the services with type semantically related to the requested type. For example, assume that we are looking for the service type 'Fixed-PhoneService', which is a semantic concept, as shown in the excerpt of the framework ontology depicted in Fig. 5.

The discovery mechanism retrieves the following matches, which are semantically related to the requested type:

i) `FixedPhoneService` $\subset$ `PhoneService` (`FixedPhoneService` is a *subsume* match of `PhoneService`)

ii) `FixedPhoneService` $\supset$ `WorkPhone` (`FixedPhoneService` is a *plug in* match of `WorkPhone`)

iii) `FixedPhoneService` $\supset$ `HomePhone` (`FixedPhoneService` is a *plug in* match of `HomePhone`)

iv) `FixedPhoneService` $\equiv$ `FixedPhoneService` (`FixedPhoneService` is *exact* match of `FixedPhoneService`)

The discovery mechanism selects the *best match* among the options above. The best match is the *exact* match, followed by the *plug in* matches and then by the *subsume* match. The *discovery web service* in Fig. 3 returns the `endpoint` of the best match to the coordinator BPEL process. We realized the publication and discovery mechanisms as web services, so that they are eventually accessible from any component of the framework. The publication and discovery mechanisms are based on the work presented in [19].

The BPEL process finishes once the service endpoint has been discovered in the jUDDI registry and the contact details of the buddy have been retrieved from the database. Endpoint and contact details are given as output to the coordinator client located in the user agent (*RequestOutputs*). Fig. 3 shows that the user agent also contains the clients to invoke the SMS, phone, e-mail and chat services (one client for each service). These are generic clients for the services, i.e., they do not have a specific service endpoint. Provided with the endpoint, the user agent can finally invoke the proper communication service (*service invocation*) and provide this service with the contact details of the buddy in order to finally put the user in contact with his/her buddy via the right communication channel.

We have performed an initial implementation of the presented components, to demonstrate its practical feasibility.

## 4   Case Study

Fig. 6 shows an example of the platform-independent service design model, which is the result of the behavioural refinements at the PIM level of our methodology. These behavioural refinements are out of the scope of this paper and are presented in [4,5].

Fig. 6 shows part of the functionality of the Live Contacts case study, namely *contactRequest*, which is described in the scenario presented in Section 3. This part of functionality involves several components, which are the user agent, the coordinator, the database, the service trader, and two action providers (the SMS and phone services). Fig. 6 uses ISDL (Interaction System Design Language) [9], which allows the specification of behavioural aspects of interacting components. Particularly, ISDL allows us to specify the control flow of each component in terms of causality relations, and the interactions between components in terms of two contributions, one for each component involved in the interaction.

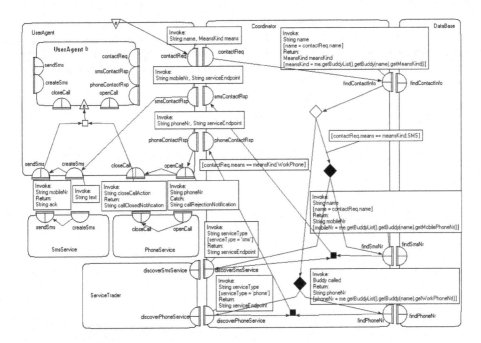

**Fig. 6.** Platform-independent service design model (exported from Grizzle [7])

Fig. 6 shows that the user request to contact a buddy with a specific communication means (*contactReq*) is forwarded by the user agent to the coordinator. This request contains two parameters, which are the name of the buddy (*name*) and the communication means to contact this buddy (*means*). The coordinator retrieves from the database the communication means available for the buddy (*findContactInfo*). Afterwards, the coordinator evaluates the parameters of the contact request. Depending on the means selected by the user (*SMS* or *WorkPhone*), a proper communication channel is selected (*SMS* or *phone*). In both cases, the coordinator performs two activities concurrently, namely, retrieving from the database the number where to contact the buddy (*findSmsNr* or *findPhoneNr*), and asking the service trader to discover the proper service to contact the buddy (*discoverSmsService* or *discoverPhoneService*). In the discovery, the coordinator indicates the service type to dicover (*sms* or *phone*), and the service trader returns the endpoint of this service (*serviceEndpoint*). Once both the service discovery and the database retrieval are concluded, the coordinator sends a response to the user agent (*smsContactRsp* or *phoneContactRsp*) with the information necessary to invoke the service, i.e., the contact details of the buddy (*mobileNr* or *phoneNr*) and the endpoint location of the service (*serviceEndpoint*). In this way, the user agent is able to invoke the proper action provider (*SmsService* or *PhoneService*) and provide it with the necessary input, which may be the mobile number or the work phone number of the buddy. We assume here that all the services published in the service trader with *serviceType = 'sms'* present the same behaviour as *SmsService* in Fig. 6. Analogously, all the services published in the service trader with *serviceType = 'phone'* present the same behaviour as *PhoneService* in Fig. 6.

We realized a prototype based on the platform-independent service design model of Fig. 6 by using the platform-specific framework described in Section 3. We experimented and tested this prototype. Fig. 7 shows the BPEL process that implements the coordinator, which orchestrates all the components of our platform-specific framework.

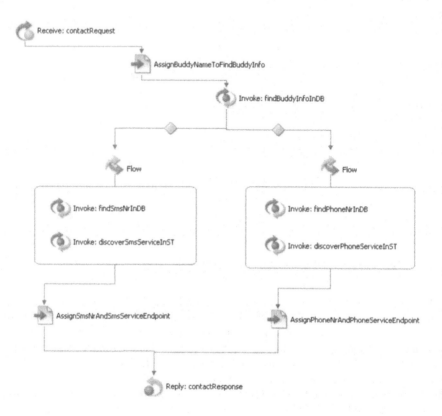

**Fig. 7.** Platform-specific service design model: the coordinator BPEL process

The BPEL process starts with a *receive* activity (*contactRequest*) that accepts as inputs the name of the buddy and the communication means to contact the buddy. The *assign* activity *AssignBuddyNameToFindBuddyInfo* copies the name of the buddy of the *contactRequest* activity to the *invoke* activity called *findBuddyInfoInDB*. This latter activity consists of an invocation of the database web service in order to retrieve the communication means available for the buddy. The BPEL process in Fig. 7 continues in two alternative flows, one in case the selected communication means is '*SMS*', and the other one in case it is '*WorkPhone*'. These flows execute two *invoke* activities in parallel: the invocation of the database service to retrieve the contact details of the buddy, and the invocation of the discovery web service to discover the endpoint of the service. When both *invoke* activities in the flow are concluded, their output is assigned to the *reply* activity (*contactResponse*) that ends the BPEL process.

The *contactResponse* activity sends the outputs of the process to the coordinator client in the user agent.

## 5   Related Work

Much effort has been done to develop SOA-based middleware solutions for context-aware services and applications [1,8,11,12]. The benefits of using SOA to support the development of such applications have been extensively discussed in the literature [2,21]. In [21], the convergence of context-awareness and service-orientation in ubiquitous computing is discussed by comparing context-awareness principles, such as *adaptation* and *extension*, to SOA principles, such as *abstraction* and *loosely coupling*. Particularly, it is shown how abstraction and loosely coupling principles in SOA support, respectively, adaptation and extension principles in context-awareness.

In [2], service-oriented context-aware application design is discussed and a service-oriented architecture that separates context parameters from application data is proposed. Although this architecture reflects the need to distinguish components devoted to context management and application core in the design of context-aware services, [2] does not describe a design process that supports this architecture. In contrast, we present a SOA-based reference architecture for context-aware mobile applications that is embedded in a comprehensive design methodology that supports the architecture.

Our design methodology is based on the MDA principles and addresses behavioural issues of model transformations in the design of the applications. These behavioural issues are usually overlooked in common MDA approaches [14]. In this paper, we show that behavioural aspects, which we have addressed already at the Platform-Independent Model (PIM) level, can be consistently realized at the Platform-Specific Model (PSM) level without any need to incorporate them later in the development process, by adding hand-written code as annotations to PSMs or to implementation code skeletons.

## 6   Conclusions and Future Work

This paper presented a prototype of a platform-specific framework for the realization of context-aware mobile applications. This prototype is one of the possible realizations with target technologies of a platform-independent model obtained through gradual behaviour model transformations of an abstract service specification. This paper shows the feasibility of this prototype. The prototype actually reflects the interoperability among components that we modelled in our design. Therefore, we can conclude that the transformation from platform-independent level to platform-specific level preserves correctness and consistency of the original behaviour of the application. However, this is only a first step towards the validation of our methodology and further work needs to be done to validate the complete design and implementation.

In this paper, we do not discuss the transformation from the platform-independent model in Fig. 6 to the platform-specific model in Fig. 7. We only provide the source and target models of this transformation. The mapping from ISDL to BPEL is part of the work presented in [6,18].

We realized only a limited part of the functionality of the Live Contacts case study, in which the coordinator handles one of the possible user request to the application. However, in the complete case study the coordinator has to handle several user requests and context events at the same time. These requests and events are realized by interacting components with different but interdependent executions threads. Therefore, the coordinator has to handle concurrency and synchronization issues of interacting components. This is part of the work presented in [5].

We provided a feasible implementation of part of our reference architecture for context-aware mobile applications. We did not consider here context source components that retrieve context information from the user environment and provide the coordinator with context events in case of changes in this context. The integration of these components in our reference architecture using a context expression evaluator is discussed in [3]. However, we envision an alternative realization of these components with web services technologies. In this work, by implementing the action providers as web services, we learned that this is a feasible and interesting solution to guarantee flexibility, interoperability and portability in our platform-specific framework. Further study needs to be performed in order to integrate context source components in the framework and expose them as web services. These components require mechanisms to allow the coordinator to dynamically subscribe to context events as soon as these components become available to the application. However, we believe that the experiments we have performed in this paper by building action providers as web services, have brought us a step forward towards the realization of context sources with this technology.

# References

1. Bai, Y., Ji, H., Han, Q., Huang, J., Qian, D.: MidCASE: A Service Oriented Middleware Enabling Context Awareness for Smart Environment. In: International Conference on Multimedia and Ubiquitous Engineering (MUE 2007), pp. 946–995. IEEE Computer Society Press, Los Alamitos (2007)
2. Chaari, T., Laforest, F., Celentano, A.: Service-Oriented Context-Aware Application Design. In: First International Workshop on Managing Context Information in Mobile and Pervasive Environments (MCMP 2005), Cyprus (2005)
3. Daniele, L., Ferreira Pires, L., van Sinderen, M.: Context Handling in a SOA Infrastructure for Context-Aware Applications. In: Proceedings of the 2nd International Workshop on Architectures, Concepts and Technologies for Service Oriented Computing (ACT4SOC 2008), Porto, Portugal, July 2008, pp. 27–37. INSTICC Press (2008)
4. Daniele, L., Ferreira Pires, L., van Sinderen, M.: An MDA-Based Approach for Behaviour Modelling of Context-Aware Mobile Applications. In: Paige, R., Hartman, A., Rensink, A. (eds.) ECMDA-FA 2009, Enschede, The Netherlands, June 2009. LNCS, vol. 5562, pp. 206–220. Springer, Heidelberg (2009)
5. Daniele, L., Ferreira Pires, L., van Sinderen, M.: Ferreira Pires. L., van Sinderen, M.: Towards Automatic Behaviour Synthesis of a Coordinator Component for Context-Aware Mobile Applications. In: Proceedings of the International Workshop on Mobile Technologies in Enterprise Computing Systems (MTECS 2009), Auckland, New Zealand, September 2009. IEEE Computer Society Press, Los Alamitos (2009)

6. Dirgahayu, T., Quartel, D., van Sinderen, M.: Development of Transformations from Business Process Models to Implementations by Reuse. In: Proceedings of the 3th International Workshop on Model-Driven Enterprise Information Systems (MDEIS 2007), Portugal, June 2007, pp. 41–50. INSTICC Press (2007)
7. Grizzle home, `http://isdl.ctit.utwente.nl/tools/grizzle`
8. Gu, T., Pung, H.K., Zhang, D.Q.: A Service-Oriented Middleware for Building Context-Aware Services. Journal of Network and Computer Applications (JNCA) 28(1) (2005)
9. ISDL home, `http://isdl.ctit.utwente.nl`
10. jUDDI home, `http://ws.apache.org/juddi`
11. Kiani, S.L., Riaz, M., Sungyoung, L., Young-Koo, L.: Context Awareness in Large Scale Ubiquitous Environments with a Service-Oriented Distributed Middleware Approach. In: 4th Annual ACIS International Conference on Computer and Information Science (ICIS 2005), pp. 513–518. IEEE Computer Society Press, Los Alamitos (2005)
12. Kim, E., Choi, J.: A Context-Awareness Middleware Based on Service-Oriented Architecture. In: Indulska, J., Ma, J., Yang, L.T., Ungerer, T., Cao, J. (eds.) UIC 2007. LNCS, vol. 4611, pp. 953–962. Springer, Heidelberg (2007)
13. Live Contacts home, `http://livecontacts.telin.nl`
14. McNeile, A., Simons, N.: Methods of Behaviour Modelling: A Commentary on Behaviour Modelling Techniques for MDA. Metamaxim Ltd home,
    `http://www.metamaxim.com/download/documents/Methods.pdf`
15. OASIS: OASIS-Commites- OASIS UDDI Specifications TC,
    `http://oasis-open.org/commitees/uddi-spec/doc/tcspecs.htm`
16. Object Management Group: MDA-Guide, Version 1.0.1, omg/03-06-01 (2003)
17. Object Management Group: Trading Object Service Specification, Version 1.0, formal/00-06-27 (2000)
18. Quartel, D., Dirgahayu, T., van Sinderen, M.: Model-Driven Design, Simulation and Implementation of Service Compositions in COSMO. Int. J. of Business Process Integration and Management (to appear)
19. Silva, E., Martínez López, J., Ferreira Pires, L., van Sinderen, M.: Defining and Prototyping a Life-cycle for Dynamic Service Composition. In: Proceedings of the 2nd Workshop on Architectures, Concepts and Technologies for Service Oriented Computing (ACT4SOC 2008), Porto, Portugal, July 2008, pp. 79–90. INSTICC Press (2008)
20. Ter Hofte, G.H., Otte, R.A.A., Kruse, H.C.J., Snijders, M.: Context-Aware Communication with Live Contacts. In: Conference Supplement of Computer Supported Cooperative Work (CSCW 2004), Chicago, USA (November 2004)
21. Yoon, H.: A Convergence of Context-Awareness and Service-Orientation in Ubiquitous Computing. International Journal of Computer Science and Network Security (IJCSNS) 7(3), 253–257 (2007)

# An Ontological Solution to Support Interoperability in the Textile Industry

Arantxa Duque[1], Cristina Campos[1],
Ernesto Jiménez-Ruiz[2], and Ricardo Chalmeta[1]

[1] Research Group on Systems Integration and Re-Engineering (IRIS)
[2] Temporal Knowledge Bases Group (TKBG)
Dept. de Llenguatges i Sistemes Informàtics, Universitat Jaume I, Castelló, Spain
{arantxa.duque,camposc,ejimenez,rchalmet}@uji.es

**Abstract.** Significant developments in information and communication technologies and challenging market conditions have forced enterprises to adapt their way of doing business. In this context, providing mechanisms to guarantee interoperability among heterogeneous organisations has become a critical issue. Even though prolific research has already been conducted in the area of enterprise interoperability, we have found that enterprises still struggle to introduce fully interoperable solutions, especially, in terms of the development and application of ontologies. Thus, the aim of this paper is to introduce basic ontology concepts in a simple manner and to explain the advantages of the use of ontologies to improve interoperability. We will also present a case study showing the implementation of an application ontology for an enterprise in the textile/clothing sector.

**Keywords:** Interoperability, Ontology, Thesaurus, Case-Study, Textile/ Clothing Industry.

## 1 Introduction

Nowadays, firms are required to work in an effective and efficient manner to create greater possibilities of success in the international market. In order to achieve this, they must collaborate with each other, and it is at this point when communication problems arise. Thus, even if the companies in collaboration belong to the same sector the differences in format or layout of documents or the business logic used, may cause the collaboration process to slow down and, in the worst case scenario, to fail, decreasing opportunities for the companies in the market. *Interoperability* enables the above mentioned problems to be resolved.

According to the IEEE association interoperability is the ability of two or more systems or components to exchange information and to use the information that has been exchanged [1].

Three main research themes or domains that address interoperability issues have been identified by the Thematic European Network IDEAS[2], namely: (1) Enterprise modelling (EM) dealing with the definition of interoperability requirements; (2) Architecture & Platform (A&P) defining implementation solutions to

R. Poler, M. van Sinderen, and R. Sanchis (Eds.): IWEI 2009, LNBIP 38, pp. 38–51, 2009.

achieve interoperability; (3) Ontologies (ONTO) addressing the semantics necessary to assure interoperability [3]. Ontologies have critical roles in support of browsing and searches for e-commerce and in support of interoperability for facilitation of knowledge management and configuration. Ontologies can be used as central controlled vocabularies that are integrated into catalogues, databases, web publications and, knowledge management applications, providing a concrete specification of term names and term meanings [4].

The purpose of this paper is to clarify ontology related concepts to researchers, managers and end users and present how ontologies can be used to support interoperability. In this paper we present a case study showing the implementation of an application ontology for a business in the textile/clothing sector that should serve as a basis of a public domain ontology. In next section we review the basic ontology related concepts and we introduce the methodology followed to develop our application ontology. Section 3 introduces the most relevant works about enterprise ontologies. Section 4 describes the main characteristics of the textile/clothing industry. In section 5, we introduce a textile thesaurus developed after the study of the domain and we describe the evolution from that thesaurus to an application ontology specially designed for the case study, a local textile/clothing company, introducing the benefits obtained from the use of ontologies for the enterprise interoperability. Finally, conclusions and future research proposals are included in section 6.

## 2   Ontology Basic Concepts

Several definitions of the concept ontology have been made, but the one by Gruber [5] is the most popular and widely accepted, and adopted in this paper: an *ontology* is an *explicit specification of a conceptualisation*.

Ontologies define the terms and common concepts used to describe and represent a particular domain or knowledge area, as well as the relationships among these terms and the rules for combining them. The choice of an ontology determines the way in which we perceive and represent our environment. Thus, ontologies are no other than a formalism for knowledge representation. This knowledge can be formalised using the following components: concepts, relations, functions, axioms and instances.

One of the most extended uses of ontologies is the support of *structured, comparative*, and *customised searches*. But ontologies are more than just that, they are also powerful tools for providing *interoperability support*. In general Interoperability projects, approaches and frameworks developed, consider as a requirement for their solution the development and use of Ontologies where terminology can be clarified for all the stakeholders as for example in [3,6,7,2,8]. In the simple case of considering controlled vocabularies, there is enhanced interoperability support since different users/applications are using the same set of terms. In simple taxonomies, we can recognise when one application is using a term that is more general or more specific than another term and facilitate interoperability. In more expressive ontologies, we may have a complete operational definition for how one term relates to another term and thus, we can use equality axioms or mappings to express one term precisely in terms of another [4].

## 2.1  Ontology Representation Formalisms

Generally, ontologies are represented in languages that allow abstraction of the low-level data modelling; in practice, ontology representation languages present an expressive power close to first order logics [5]. This capacity for abstraction is what allows ontologies to support interoperability.

Figure 1 presents the existing formalisms for knowledge specification according to their semantic expressiveness. Genuine lexical resources are placed closer to the left, while more formal ontologies are at the right end of the spectrum. We consider a *lexicon* as a compilation of domain terms. A *thesaurus* is no other than a lexicon that includes basic relationships between concepts and, generally, classifies those terms within a hierarchy. On the other hand, *domain ontologies* integrate complex rules and axioms concerning a particular case of application.

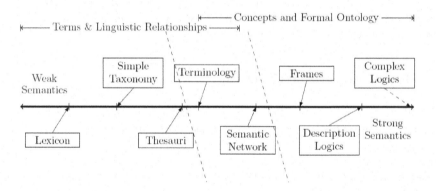

**Fig. 1.** Adapted Ontology Spectrum based on [4,9,10]

Lexical knowledge (i.e. lexicons, thesauri) has been integrated into ontologies in different ways. In the simplest approach, it is introduced directly as one of the properties of the concept. Even though the previous scenario seems to be the preferred one by the community, authors in [9,10] propose that ontologies and lexical resources (thesauri in our case) to be kept separated from each other. This organisation enables the reuse of a thesauri by several resources within the same domain. This reuse may improve ontology alignment since ontology concepts will be linked to entries of the same thesaurus. Figure 2 shows such linkage between ontology concepts and thesaurus terms. If the same entry in the thesaurus is linked to several ontology concepts, this may indicate that these concepts are potentially aligned.

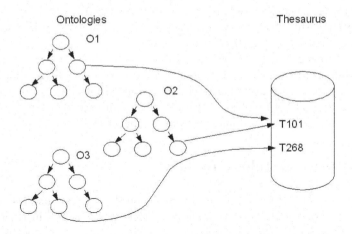

**Fig. 2.** Ontology thesaurus link based on [10]

## 2.2   Ontology Development Methodologies

There are several design criteria and development approach methodologies for Ontologies, including those proposed by Natasha Noy et al [11], Uschold and Gruninger [12], Guarino [13],and A. Gomez-Perez et al [14].

All these methods focus, in particular, on scenarios where a harmonisation between similar ontologies is required or there is a need to achieve the interoperability of distributed knowledge sources, which may be either databases or ontologies or both.

*INTEROP* Network of Excellence [6] adopts UPON (Unified Process for ONtology building) [15]. UPON is an incremental methodology for ontology building that takes into account that in most cases companies require a migration of the already existing knowledge bases (typically relational databases) to ontologies; and generally these existing knowledge bases would still continue to exist and need to interoperate with the newly designed ontology as well.

UPON's characteristics stem from the Software Development Unified Process, one of the most widespread and accepted methods in the software engineering community, and it uses the Unified Modelling Language (UML) to support the preparation of all the blueprints of the ontology project.

What distinguishes UPON from other methodologies, for software and ontology engineering respectively, is their *use-case driven, iterative* and *incremental* nature. UPON presents cycles, phases, iterations and workflows. Each cycle consists of four phases (inception, elaboration, construction and transition) and results in the release of a new version of the ontology. Each phase is further subdivided into iterations.

For each iteration five workflows take place: requirements, analysis, design, implementation and test; and a richer and more complete version of the target ontology is produced. The incremental nature of UPON first requires the identification of relevant terms in the domain, gathered into a lexicon; then this is progressively enriched with definitions, yielding a glossary; adding the basic ontological relationships to it allows a thesaurus to be produced, until, with further enrichments, it takes a final shape.

The methodologies for ontology design mentioned above have many points in common, but in this paper we will mainly focus on the UPON methodology as we consider that its iterative nature is more appropriate and adapts better to our domain and case study. But, as we mentioned already in this paper, we will keep the thesaurus and the domain ontology separated from each other.

# 3   Enterprise Ontology Review

*Enterprise Ontology* (EO) has its origins in the need to develop models at a high-level of abstraction with the development of effective inter- and intra-enterprise information systems. These models need to be understood by both business people, who are defining their functionality, and software engineers, who are constructing and implementing the software systems that realise the systems' functionality. The idea of business components for modelling information systems is very valuable since they directly reflect the business rules and the constraints that apply to the enterprise domain [16].

Thus, an Enterprise Ontology is a collection of terms, definitions, relations and rules relevant to business enterprises. In order to develop an enterprise ontology, all the terms in the business need to be considered and clearly defined. This includes the company's intended purposes, the processes and everything happening in the business. From the research of AIAI (Artificial Intelligence Applications Institute in the University of Edinburgh) the main uses for the Enterprise Ontology include to [17]:

- *Enhance communication* between humans, for the benefit of integration.
- Serve as stable *basis for understanding* and specifying the requirements for end-user applications, which leads to more flexibility in an organisation.
- *Achieve interoperability* among disparate tools in an enterprise modelling environment using the EO as an interchange format.

## 3.1   Enterprise Ontology Approaches

TOVE (TOronto Virtual Enterprise) ontology is the result of the TOVE [18] project conducted by the University of Toronto. The TOVE project provides a generic, reusable data model that provides a shared terminology for the business and enterprise.

The researchers in the National Institute of Standards and Technology developed PSL (Process Specification Languages) [19]. PSL, initially based on TOVE, identifies, formally defines, and structures the semantic concepts intrinsic to the capture and exchange of discrete manufacturing process information.

Finally, the Edinburgh Enterprise Ontology or the Enterprise Ontology (EO) [17] project's goal is to provide "a collection of terms and definitions relevant to business enterprises to enable coping with a fast changing environment through improved business planning, greater flexibility, more effective communication and integration". The EO project has also developed tools for modelling, communicating and representing enterprises and processes in a unique way. The EO is represented in an informal way (text version) and in a formal language (Ontolingua).

All these efforts offer a great contribution to ontology development as a support mechanism for interoperability. But, in real life, only large companies can afford these solutions. In fact, a large number of enterprises have a very poor understanding of what ontologies and their advantages are. Moreover, even though a huge amount of information about ontologies and their applications has been written, the number of tangible or free-accessible ontologies is very scarce.

The aim of this paper is make all this information accessible to the general public and provide the reader with a practical and simple example of how an application ontology can be designed and implemented. More precisely, we will focus on the design of an application ontology for a local textile/clothing company.

## 4   Case Study Context

Because the aim of this document is to present an application ontology developed for a textile/clothing enterprise, we will now briefly review the main characteristics of this sector and describe the most significant research conducted to introduce interoperable solutions in the domain.

### 4.1   About the Textile/Clothing Industry

The production process within the Textile/Clothing sector is based on collaboration between a large number of small and medium enterprises (SMEs) to create and deliver items of textiles and clothing. Each of these enterprises is responsible for a particular aspect of the production process: such co-operation is regulated by the exchange of request/response messages necessary to carry out all the steps in the supply chain. The delivery timing of the final product is affected by the communication mechanism adopted within the supply chain. In this sector the introduction of fully interoperable solutions and standards is a harder task when compared to other production processes, since the sophistication and specificity of the cooperation among the enterprises of the supply chain (mainly based on human relationships instead of Information and Communication Technologies) are very high and represent a peculiar competitive factor.

### 4.2   Textile/Clothing Industry Interoperability Approaches Review

Up until 2000, most innovation was aimed at automating internal business processes. In many cases, even this was usually only within individual departments, leaving inter-enterprise processes as manual. The only existing interoperability solutions were based on EDIFACT [20] technology, and EDITEX [21], which are described below.

The EDI, Electronic Data Interchange, defined by a UN Commission, was focused on the simplification of international commerce. It was based on:(1)A document structure for international electronic commerce; (2) the UN dictionary of the words for international trade; and (3)the ISO syntax for the electronic transfer of data within flat files. The result was a rigid technology, EDIFACT, where customisations were made by suppressing of unused parts of a common general structure. This approach was valuable because it conveys a universal standard, but it was only affordable for large organisations.

In the period between 1980 and 1990, the EDITEX project developed the EDIFACT subsets for the European Textile and Clothing industry. Despite these efforts, the diffusion of the EDITEX solution was also limited to a few very large organisations.

*eTexML* [22] is a French project coordinated by the *Institut Francais du Textiles et de l'Habillement* - IFTH. The project was initiated in order to provide a set of EDI tools based on XML to allow manufacturers and retailers to implement a reactive delivery strategy.

TEX-WEAVE [23], *Standardisation and interoperability in the Textile Supply Chain Integrated Networks*, is an international project in which AITEX (*Instituto Tecnológico Textil*) [24] based in Alcoi (Spain) is involved. The aim of this project is to provide the Textile/Clothing sector with a framework for interoperability based on standardised electronic document exchange based on XML Schemas.

*Moda-ML* [25] (now denominated *Moda-ML initiative*) was a European project based in Italy. The project objective was to facilitate the exchange of technical and managerial information between the companies of a supply chain in the Textile/Clothing sector. The project is especially focused on the relationship between textile providers and clothing manufacturers.

Regarding semantic-like interoperability, Moda-ML represents an interesting initiative to provide semantics for the e-business vocabulary [26,27]. They carried out the following steps based on UPON methodology: they started by identifying the necessary vocabulary terms (i.e. lexicon), then they created a basic organisation of the terms (i.e. thesaurus), and finally they automatically built an ontology following a set of patterns and descriptions extracted from a database.

The next section presents our case study, which is a study we carried out of the main requirements for developing a reference vocabulary and ontology. As Moda-ML, we have followed a three-steps approach: definition of term requirements (i.e. lexicon), analysis and organisation of terms (i.e. thesaurus), and implementation of a formalisation (i.e. ontology).

# 5    Development of an Ontology for the Textile/Clothing Industry

The case study is an enterprise involved in the hosiery and textile/clothing industry. The company expanded and diversified its operations to also manufacture socks and to produce all its own yarn and fibre requirements. The company has kept growing and introduced new product areas such as underwear, beachwear, pyjamas and lingerie.

For the sake of brevity, in this paper we will focus on the part of the ontology developed to describe the technical specifications or characteristics of the wide range of products manufactured and commercialised by the company.

Next we will describe the steps conducted in order to complete our ontology, based on the UPON methodology described in subsection 2.2,. Figure 3 shows how UPON methodology has been adapted to our particular case of study.

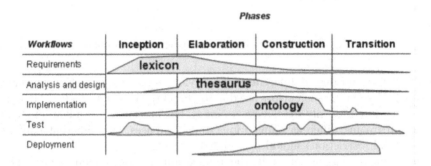

**Fig. 3.** Steps conducted in order to develop our application ontology based on [15,28]

## 5.1    Determine the Domain, the Benefits and the Scope of the Ontology

During this phase of the study it is vital to determine what the domain of the ontology is, what the ontology will be used for and who will use and maintain the ontology.

After a precise study of the enterprise to gain a deep understanding of its workflow, we decided to focus our ontology on the *textile products* that are produced and marketed.

It is improtant to determine how the company would benefit from the development of an application ontology. The most immediate and evident advantage is the possibility of introducing *semantic searches* on the enterprise web portal from which employees and customers would benefit.

The creation of the ontology and the introduction of a shared thesaurus for the domain can also provide interoperability support. As shown in Figure 4, ontologies can be used to formally abstract the knowledge represented in a particular database. Additionally, if these ontologies share a domain thesaurus, interoperability support is enhanced since different users/applications are using the same set of terms; moreover, mappings between them can be directly defined.

Regarding the semantic integration, ontologies can also be used to detect incompatibilities between database schemas to be integrated. When merging independently developed ontologies, given a set of mappings between them, errors

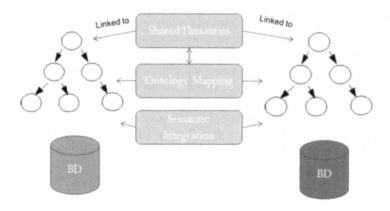

**Fig. 4.** Use of ontologies to support interoperability

are likely to occur due to different points of view in the respective conceptualisations [29]. In general such errors are due to global restrictions which are not true in all contexts (e.g. only *items* have a *name*), but in a specific application. Thus, when integrating different applications and databases with different contexts, these global restrictions should be avoided.

In our particular case of study, the application ontology enhances internal interoperability between the different departments of the company since they now have a shared domain thesaurus defining the most common terms. A specific ontology could also be developed for each department. This particular ontology should take into account the most relevant processes of every unit. Moreover, a mapping between these ontologies may also be implemented. Thus, the shared thesaurus and the set of departmental ontologies will provide a fully interoperable solution within the company.

On the other hand, external Enterprise Interoperability could be also achieved by providing the enterprises that usually collaborate with the company under study with ontological solutions based on our shared thesaurus. This will allow local companies to cooperate with each other in a more effective and efficient manner.

## 5.2   Identification of Relevant Terms

Once the scope and the domain of the ontology have been clearly defined, the next step is to identify the relevant terms in the application domain (i.e. the *lexicon*), the textile/clothing sector in our case of study, and elaborate a lexicon including the most general terms.

In order to achieve this, we studied and analysed several clothing catalogues from the most important companies in the sector. We especially focused on nightwear, hosiery, socks and underwear, as they are the main items commercialised by our case study. The result of this study was a compilation of the domain's most relevant terms (see Figure 5). Some of the concepts included in our lexicon are *Brand, Colour, Size, Fabric, Item, Season, Collection*, etc.

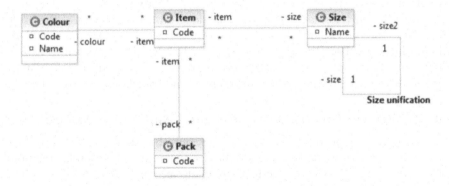

**Fig. 5.** UML representation of a subset of the domain concepts

## 5.3  Introduction of Basic Relationships between Terms

The next step after the lexicon development is the introduction of the basic relationships between domain concepts to obtain a *thesaurus*. As mentioned in section one, this thesaurus will ideally be shared among different companies in the sector or different departments within a company and it will be the foundation for the development of an application ontology reflecting the particularities of each individual enterprise in the textile sector. By basic relationships between domain concepts, we understand: the classification of the domain concepts within a hierarchy and establishment of linguistic relationships such as synonyms and translations. In our thesaurus, for example, terms are defined in English and Spanish and an equivalence between the sizes used in different countries has been introduced.

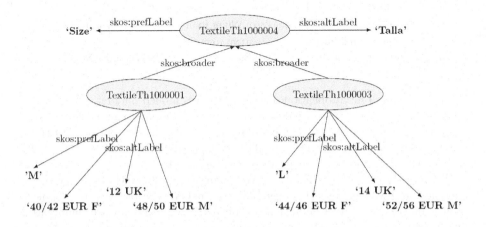

**Fig. 6.** Excerpt from the developed SKOS-like Thesaurus

We have used SKOS (Simple Knowledge Organization System) [30,31] as a formal language to represent our *textile thesaurus* (**TextileTh**). This language has a rich support for labelling and reporting term metadata (e.g. Preferred label, Alternate labels, definitions, examples) as well as for defining linguistic relationships (e.g. Has Broader, Has Narrower, Related, Exact Match). Figure 6 shows an example of a set of SKOS-like entries organised within a hierarchy (skos:broader) and showing different synonyms and translations (skos:altLabel).

### 5.4   Design and Creation of the Required Application Axioms

Once we have developed a domain thesaurus, our objective is now to introduce the required axioms to model the particular business rules and complex relationships between the case study products to create an *application ontology*. Thus, we will create the enterprise's application ontology taking the shared domain thesaurus as a reference.

**Table 1.** Excerpt from the product definition required in the case

**XS and S are small sizes**

$\alpha_1$    $Small\_Sizes \equiv XS \sqcup S$

**XL, XXL and XXXL are big sizes**

$\alpha_2$    $Big\_Sizes \equiv XL \sqcup XXL \sqcup XXL$

**A Pack includes two or more items with the same Size**

$\alpha_3$    $Item\_S \equiv Item \sqcap \exists hasSize.S \sqcap \forall hasSize.S$

$\alpha_4$    $Pack\_S \equiv Pack \sqcap \forall hasItem.Item\_S \sqcap \geqslant 2\, hasItem.Item\_S$

$\alpha_5$    $Pack \equiv Pack\_S \sqcup Pack\_XS \sqcup \ldots \sqcup Pack\_XL \sqcup Pack\_XXL \sqcup Pack\_XXXL$

**A Basic Pack includes three items: 1 black, 1 white and 1 ecru**

$\alpha_6$    $White\_Item \equiv Item \sqcap \exists hasColour.White \sqcap \forall hasColour.White$

$\alpha_7$    $Black\_Item \equiv Item \sqcap \exists hasColour.Black \sqcap \forall hasColour.Black$

$\alpha_8$    $Ecru\_Item \equiv Item \sqcap \exists hasColour.Ecru \sqcap \forall hasColour.Ecru$

$\alpha_9$    $PackBasic\_S \equiv Pack\_S \sqcap \exists hasItem.White\_Item \sqcap \exists hasItem.Black\_Item$
        $\sqcap \exists hasItem.Ecru\_Item \sqcap\, = 3\, hasItem.Item\_S$

$\alpha_{10}$    $PackBasic \equiv PackBasic\_S \sqcup PackBasic\_XS \sqcup \ldots \sqcup PackBasic\_XXXL$

The creation of an application ontology requires a deep understanding of the business rules, processes and particularities of the company you are developing the ontology for. In order to fully understand how the enterprise works, we arranged several meetings with the different departments involved in the design and commercialisation of their products, including IT.

We have adopted OWL (Ontology Web Language) [32,33,34] as the ontology language, and we have used Protégé 4 [35] as the OWL ontology editor. Table 1 shows some of the product definition specifications required they are enumerated in English, but their formal representation using description logics [36] is also included.

# 6   Conclusions

Theoretically, there is no doubt about the benefits of using ontologies to support enterprise interoperability and to facilitate the development of the semantic web. The aim of this research is to clarify ontology related concepts to companies and end users, so they can benefit from the actual application of these mechanisms. Moreover, in this paper we have presented a practical approach to ontology design and development by introducing an application ontology for the textile sector, that should be the beginning for a development of a public ontology in this sector.

The main problem encountered during our research is that even though there have been plenty of efforts in the last few years to develop a textile thesaurus that could be used as a standard in this domain, nowadays, few companies are aware of the actual benefits of investing in these mechanisms and using them as tools to support interoperability. In this paper, we have developed a simplified thesaurus for the sector that could be the foundation for the creation of a standard. Moreover, we have introduced how an application ontology can be developed, taking this thesaurus as a reference. Even today, the creation of a standard thesaurus is necessary for the future development and actual use of application ontologies within the textile sector.

Thus, we can conclude that there is still a lot to do before the actual use of application ontologies in the textile/clothing industry. As we have already mentioned, the main reason for this is the lack of a standard thesaurus or taxonomy collecting the domain relevant concepts and basic relationships. We also consider it is very important to carry out initiatives to educate companies and employees in the use of ontologies, and to prove to them that they can benefit from these mechanisms. Practical examples of use may be introduced so enterprises can better understand how the use of ontologies can enhance communications with customers, suppliers and stakeholders.

**Acknowledgments.** This work was partially funded by CICYT DPI2006-14708, BPI06/372 and IMPIVA.

# References

1. IEEE Computer Society Press: IEEE standard computer dictionary: a compilation of IEEE standard computer glossaries, New York, NY, USA (January 1991)
2. IDEAS: Interoperability Development for Enterprise Application and Software Project (2005), http://www.ideas-roadmap.net
3. Chen, D., Doumeingts, G.: European initiatives to develop interoperability of enterprise applications-basic concepts, framework and roadmap. Annual Reviews in Control 27(2), 153–162 (2003)
4. Mcguinness, D.L.: Ontologies come of age. In: The Semantic Web: Why, What, and How. MIT Press, Cambridge (2003)

5. Gruber, T.R.: Towards Principles for the Design of Ontologies Used for Knowledge Sharing. In: Guarino, N., Poli, R. (eds.) Formal Ontology in Conceptual Analysis and Knowledge Representation (1993),
   http://tomgruber.org/writing/ontology-definition-2007.htm
6. Bourrières, J.P.: The interop network of excellence. In: Interoperability of Enterprise Software and Applications, pp. 455–457. Springer, London (2006)
7. ATHENA: Advanced Technologies for interoperability of Heterogeneous Enterprise Networks and their Applications IP (IST-2001- 507849) (2008),
   http://www.athena-ip.org
8. Campos, C., Martí, I., Grangel, R., Mascherpa, A., Chalmeta, R.: A methodological proposal for the development of an interoperability framework. In: Model Driven Interoperability for Sustainable Information Systems (MDISIS 2008) (CAiSE 2008). CEUR-WS, vol. 340, pp. 47–57 (2008)
9. Jimeno-Yepes, A., Jimenez-Ruiz, E., Berlanga, R., Rebholz-Schuhmann, D.: Use of shared lexical resources for efficient ontological engineering. In: Semantic Web Applications and Tools for Life Sciences Workshop (SWAT4LS). CEUR WS Proceedings, vol. 435 (2008)
10. Jimeno-Yepes, A., Jimenez-Ruiz, E., Berlanga, R., Rebholz-Schuhmann, D.: Reuse of terminological resources for efficient ontological engineering in life sciences. BMC Bioinformatics (to be published, 2009)
11. Noy, N.F., Mcguinness, D.: Ontology development 101: A guide to creating your first ontology. Stanford KSL Technical Report KSL-01-05 (2000),
    http://www.ksl.stanford.edu/people/dlm/papers/ontology101/
    ontology101-noy-mcguinness.html
12. Uschold, M., Grüninger, M., Gruninger, M.: Ontologies: Principles, methods and applications. Knowledge Engineering Review 11, 93–136 (1996)
13. Guarino, N., Carrara, M., Giaretta, P.: Formalizing ontological commitments. In: AAAI 1994: Proceedings of the twelfth national conference on Artificial intelligence, vol. 1, pp. 560–567. American Association for Artificial Intelligence, Menlo Park (1994)
14. Fernandez-Lopez, M., Gomez-Perez, A., Juristo, N.: METHONTOLOGY: from ontological art towards ontological engineering. In: Proceedings of the AAAI 1997 Spring Symposium, Stanford, USA, March 1997, pp. 33–40 (1997)
15. Nicola, A.D., Missikoff, M., Navigli, R.: A proposal for a unified process for ontology building: Upon. In: Andersen, K.V., Debenham, J., Wagner, R. (eds.) DEXA 2005. LNCS, vol. 3588, pp. 655–664. Springer, Heidelberg (2005)
16. Albani, A., Dietz, J.L.G.: The benefit of enterprise ontology in identifying business components. In: The Past and Future of Information Systems: 1976–2006 and Beyond. IFIP International Federation for Information Processing, vol. 214, pp. 243–484. Springer, Boston (2006)
17. Uschold, M., King, M., Moralee, S., Zorgios, Y., Uschold, M., King, M., House, S.B.R., Moralee, S., Zorgios, Y.: The enterprise ontology. The Knowledge Engineering Review 13, 31–89 (1998)
18. TOVE: Toronto Virtual Enterprise project. Enterprise Modelling,
    http://www.eil.utoronto.ca/enterprise-modelling/index.html
19. PSL: NIST Process Specification Language, http://www.mel.nist.gov/psl/
20. EDIFACT: Electronic Data Interchange For Administration, Commerce and Transport, http://www.unece.org/cefact/
21. EDITEX: TEDIS project, Trade EDI Systems Programme. Interim report. Office for official publications of the European Community (1992) ISBN-92-826-5658-6

22. Robinet, P., Dufour, J.M., H.L.Q.: Description of the eTeXML project. Annex 8 to TEX-SPIN D10-CWA (2003)
23. TEX-WEAVE: Standardisation and Interoperability in the Textile Supply Chain Integrated Networks, http://www.texweave.org/
24. AITEX: Instituto Tecnológico Textil, http://www.aitex.es/index.php
25. Moda-ML: Public reports, http://www.moda-ml.org/moda-ml/download/documentazione/pubb_modaml. asp
26. Gessa, N., Busanelli, M., Sabbata, P.D., Vitali, F.: Extracting a semantic view from an ebusiness vocabulary. In: Proceedings of IEEE International Conference on E-Commerce Technology, pp. 398–401 (2006)
27. de Sabbata, P., Gessa, N., Busanelli, M., Brutti, A., Frascella, A.: Providing a semantic description for an interoperability framework using ontologies. In: Exploiting the knowledge economy: issues, applications, case studies, pp. 197–204. IOS Press, Amsterdam (2006)
28. Michele Missikoff, D.F.: Basic ontological solutions for interoperability. Deliverable DO1 INTEROP Network of Excellence (2006)
29. Jimenez-Ruiz, E., Cuenca Grau, B., Horrocks, I., Berlanga, R.: Ontology integration using mappings: Towards getting the right logical consequences. In: Proc. of European Semantic Web Conference (ESWC). LNCS, vol. 5554, pp. 173–187 (2009), Technical Report, http://krono.act.uji.es/people/Ernesto/contentmap
30. SKOS: Simple Knowledge Organization System, http://www.w3.org/2004/02/skos/intro
31. Miles, A., Matthews, B., Beckett, D., Brickley, D., Wilson, M., Rogers, N.: Skos: A language to describe simple knowledge structures for the web. In: Proc. of the XTech Conference: XML, the Web and beyond (2005)
32. OWL: Ontology web language, http://www.w3.org/2007/OWL/wiki/Syntax
33. Horrocks, I., Patel-Schneider, P.F., van Harmelen, F.: From $\mathcal{SHIQ}$ and RDF to OWL: the making of a web ontology language. J. Web Sem. 1(1), 7–26 (2003)
34. Cuenca Grau, B., Horrocks, I., Motik, B., Parsia, B., Patel-Schneider, P., Sattler, U.: OWL 2: The next step for OWL. J. Web Semantics 6(4), 309–322 (2008)
35. Protégé: Ontology Editor, http://protege.stanford.edu/
36. Baader, F., Calvanese, D., Mcguinness, D.L., Nardi, D., Patel-Schneider, P.F.: The description logic handbook: theory, implementation, and applications. Cambridge University Press, New York (2003)

# An Approach towards Enterprise Interoperability Assessment

Mahsa Razavi[1] and Fereidoon Shams Aliee[2]

[1] Islamic Azad University, Central Tehran Branch, Poonak, Tehran, Iran
Mahsa_r_d@yahoo.com
[2] Shahid Beheshti University, G.C., Tehran, Iran
F_shams@sbu.ac.ir

**Abstract.** Enterprise Architecture (EA) as a discipline with numerous and enterprise-wide models, can support decision making on enterprise-wide issues. In order to provide such support, EA models should be amenable to analysis of various utilities and quality attributes. This paper provides a method towards EA interoperability analysis. This approach is based on Analytical Hierarchy Process (AHP) and considers the situation of the enterprise in giving weight to the different criteria and sub criteria of each utility. It proposes a quantitative method of assessing Interoperability achievement of different scenarios using AHP based on the knowledge and experience of EA experts and domain experts, and helps in deciding between them. The applicability of the proposed approach is demonstrated using a practical case study.

**Keywords:** Enterprise Architecture, Interoperability, Quality attribute, Assessment.

## 1 Introduction

Enterprises are complex, highly integrated systems comprised of processes, organizations, information and supporting technologies, with multifaceted interdependencies and interrelationships across their boundaries. Understanding, engineering, and managing these complex social, technical, and infrastructure dimensions are critical to achieving and sustaining enterprise performance [1]. In order to provide such support, Enterprise Architecture (EA) has been emerged. Taking a holistic approach, EA focuses not only on the technical aspects but also on the various aspects of the enterprise upon which the IT systems operate [2].

As enterprise complexity rises there are many more possibilities to consider in designing an optimal enterprise, and so importance of architecting grows.

Through the emphasis on architecting, we look not just at transition from an 'as is' to the 'to be' state, but also at the underlying decision analysis related to considering the various alternative 'could be' states of the new (or transforming) enterprise.

Moreover, because the risk and impact of EA are pervasive across the enterprise, it is critical to perform an architecture assessment before any decision about choosing a scenario.

R. Poler, M. van Sinderen, and R. Sanchis (Eds.): IWEI 2009, LNBIP 38, pp. 52–65, 2009.

The enterprises of this century are truly systems in themselves and as such the properties and design issues for complex systems also relate to complex enterprises. In this field, one of the new research trends is about the way various properties and behaviors of systems relate to enterprises, and how decisions on 'could be' architecture alternatives may be made based on optimization around a given property.

Considering EA, we generally believe that quality attributes (properties) of an enterprise are primarily achieved through EA (same as software architecture [3]). In other words, most of the design decisions embodied by EA are strongly influenced by the need to achieve quality attributes.

One of the important quality attributes of an enterprise is interoperability.

Interoperability is still a vague concept and has many definitions and connotations to different people in different sectors and domains. Starting from a pure software problem in the middle of 90's, interoperability is taking on a wider meaning to cover the many knowledge spaces, dimensions and layers of single and collaborating enterprises [4].

There exist numerous definitions of interoperability, examples from literature are:

- Ability of two or more systems or components to exchange information and to use the information that has been exchanged [5]
- (computer science) the ability to exchange and use information (usually in a large heterogeneous network made up of several local area networks [6])
- Interoperability may occur between two (or more) entities that are related to one another in one of three ways [7]
    o Integrated: where there is a standard format for all constituent systems
    o Unified: where there is a common meta-level structure across constituent models, providing a means for establishing semantic equivalence
    o Federated: where models must be dynamically accommodated rather than having a predetermined meta-model
- Generally speaking, interoperability is the capability for two (or more) systems to exchange information [5] and to use reciprocally their functionality.

Although much the same, here we focus on the last (most general) definition.

Since a decade, although some efforts have been made to develop enterprise interoperability, especially in Europe [8], [9], [10] where several research projects have been launched under FP5/FP6, there is still not an overall satisfactory solution on interoperability. Research in this area is still fragmented. Most of researches and developments are focused on the technology aspect to solve interoperability problems. Few approaches are developed to evaluate the degree of interoperability.

The aim of this paper is to propose a quantitative assessment method of EA interoperability achievement for different EA scenarios, based on the enterprise's situation.

In this approach, a specialized weight is assigned to each interoperability criteria and sub-criteria according to the areas of focus in the enterprise. This is done by using the knowledge of a group of EA experts and a group of domain experts. The proposed approach uses AHP for assessing the level of interoperability of each scenario and helps enterprises compare and decide about different scenarios according to the level of interoperability they provide.

As mentioned above, the method in this paper has the additional benefit that the identification of which architecture to use is based on the situation of the enterprise and also the experience of groups of EA and domain experts. The participants are forced to systematically consider all possible combinations. This ensures a broader decision base. Moreover, it allows discussions to be held focusing on the areas where the participants' experiences differ.

The term "EA scenario" is used to denote an architecture, an architecture proposal, or a solution for an enterprise, which can be on any level of granularity. But of course the architecture scenario candidates to be compared should have the same level of granularity.

The case study provided at the end of this paper is an abbreviated version of a study under development in Ports and Maritime Organization of Iran (PMO). This is done to give a more comprehensive presentation of how the method can be used and to demonstrate the efficacy of our approach.

## 1.1   Related Work

In this part we introduce the related work to this research that consists of 3 groups:

1.  Analysis methods and tools for software quality, including the Software Ar-
    chitecture Analysis Method (SAAM) [11], the Architecture Tradeoff Analy-
    sis Method (ATAM) [12], Abd-Allah and Gacek [13], Wright [14] and the
    Chiron-2 Software Architecture Description and Evolution Language
    (C2SADEL) [15]. None of these methods are applicable in the EA domain
    [10]. These methods focus on evaluating a single software architecture to
    find out if and where there may be problems in it, while the method in this
    paper is more aimed towards finding out which EA scenario candidate, of a
    set of EA scenario candidates, has the most potential to support the mix of
    quality attributes for a particular enterprise to build.
2.  Software quality attribute measurement methods based on MCDM methods,
    including [16], [17], [18], [19], [20], [21], [22], [23] and [24].
        These methods focus on prioritizing and selecting the most appropriate
    software architecture candidate that supports the desired quality attributes. In
    this paper, we extended the idea of these methods in the EA domain.
3.  The analysis methods in the EA community including [25], [26], [27], [28],
    [29], [30], [31] and [32].
        The main contributions of our approach which makes it different from the
    above mentioned approaches of group 3 are as below:
    1.  In our approach, the criteria and sub-criteria of a quality attribute are
        given different weights according to the EA layers each of them belong
        to and also the importance of each EA layer in the enterprise. Above
        mentioned approaches, use causal effect and probability theory, and

model causal probabilities between quality attributes and criteria. The problem, however, with causal probabilities is that these are more time consuming to find and define in the EA models (compared to weights).

2.  Through our approach, we use the knowledge and experience of two groups of experts in our assessment; EA experts and domain experts. This ensures a broader decision base according to different points of view and allows identification of differences in participants' experiences.

3.  All above methods use formal languages such as Influence Diagrams or their extended version to support the analysis of EA, but we have used Analytical Hierarchy Process (AHP) as a multi criteria decision making method, which is the first experience of using this method in the field of EA assessment.

### 1.2  Outline of Paper

The remainder of the paper is outlined as follows:

Section 2 is devoted to the explanation of the proposed interoperability assessment method in a step by step manner. In section 3, we present a case study where the proposed method is used. Finally in section 4 the paper is concluded and future work are introduced.

## 2  The Proposed Interoperability Assessment Method

The objective of this paper is to help the decision makers of an enterprise to decide about different scenarios according to their level of interoperability achievement.

This method can be used when making any decision about EA issues in the enterprise in each of the phases of Target EA Design, Transition Planning and development and EA maintenance. In other words, this method is usable after gathering complete information about the current EA of the enterprise.

In this approach, we have classified interoperability measures as several criteria and sub-criteria using [4].

The approach uses Analytical Hierarchy Process (AHP) for analysis and prioritization of different elements. Different methods may be applied for prioritization [33]. This includes subjective judgment with or without consensus building and methods such as providing a total sum of points to be divided between the items or aspects you would like to prioritize. Most methods have however weaknesses and it is mostly hard to judge the goodness of the prioritization. AHP addresses some of these problems [34], since it allows for a calculation of a consistency index for the prioritization. This opportunity arises from the fact that AHP is based on all pair-wise comparisons of whatever we would like to prioritize.

To better understand the proposed approach, we first precisely describe AHP and then explain the proposed approach in a step by step manner (Fig. 1).

In this figure the boxes with thick border represent the steps that directly use AHP.

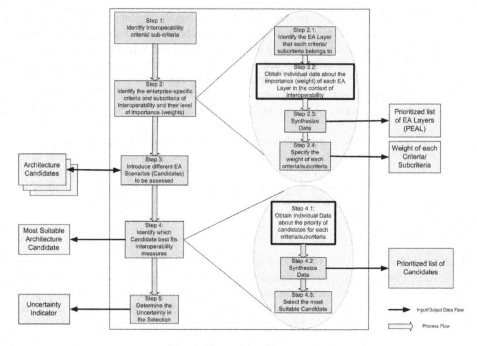

**Fig. 1.** Illustration of Solution

## 2.1 Analytical Hierarchy Process (AHP)

AHP, originally proposed by Saaty 1980 [34] is one of the multi criteria decision making methods, which is available from the management science literature. Briefly, AHP consists of a set of steps, where all combinations of elements are evaluated pairwise, and according to a certain scale. The question to answer for each pair-wise comparison is which of the two elements, i or j is more important, and how much more important is it?. This is rated by interpreting the values as presented in Table 1.

These comparisons are then transferred into a matrix, where n is the number of elements, together with the reciprocal values. After this is done, the eigenvector of the matrix is computed. [34] and [35] propose a method called averaging over normalized columns to do this. This results in an estimation of the eigenvalues of the matrix, and is called the priority vector. The priority vector is the primary output of applying AHP.

After constructing all required pairwise judgment matrices between criteria and alternatives levels, for each, the consistency ratio (CR) should be calculated. The deviation from consistency, the measure of inconsistency, is called the consistency index (CI) and is calculated using the following equation:

$$CI = \frac{\lambda_{max} - n}{n - 1} \tag{1}$$

where n is matrix size and $\lambda_{max}$ is the maximum eigenvalue of the matrix.

The CR is used to estimate directly the consistency of pairwise comparisons, and computed by dividing the CI by a value obtained from a table of random consistency index (RI), the average index for randomly generated weights [34], as shown in the following equation:

$$CR = \frac{CI}{RI} \qquad (2)$$

A consistency ratio of 0.10 or less is considered acceptable even if it is pointed out that higher values are often obtained [34] [35].

Note that if the AHP hierarchy has multiple levels of criteria and sub-criteria, the above computations must be done for each sub-criteria (leaf node of the hierarchy) and then the priority vectors of the alternatives according to each sub-criteria are synthesized into one priority vector [36]. This vector provides the final priorities of the alternatives according to the specified criteria and sub-criteria. A more extensive description of AHP can be found in e.g. [34] and [35].

**Table 1.** Scale for pairwise comparison using AHP [34][35]

| Relative Intensity | Definition | Explanation |
|---|---|---|
| 1 | Of equal importance | The two variables (i and j) are of equal importance |
| 3 | Slightly more important | One variable is slightly more important than the other |
| 5 | Highly more important | One variable is highly more important than the other |
| 7 | Very highly more important | One variable is very highly more important than the other |
| 9 | Extremely more important | One variable is extremely more important than the other |
| 2,4,6,8 | Immediate values | Used when compromising between the other numbers |
| Reciprocal | If variable i has one of the above numbers assigned to it when compared with variable j, then variable j has the value 1/number assigned to it when compared with variable I. More formally if $n_{ij}=x$ then $n_{ji}=1/x$ | |

## 2.2 Steps of the Proposed Approach

In the proposed framework, AHP is used in steps 2.2 and 4.1. It must be regarded that in each of these steps, after AHP computation (according to section 2.1), the consistency ratio (CR) of the pairwise comparisons should be computed to determine the reliability of the results. Whenever CR is more than 10%, pairwise comparison should be done again with more precise information or by other participants with more experience.

### Step 1: Identify interoperability criteria/sub-criteria
As mentioned before, in this paper we have used enterprise interoperability measures mentioned in [4] as EA interoperability criteria and sub-criteria. The hierarchy of interoperability criteria/sub-criteria is demonstrated in Fig. 2.

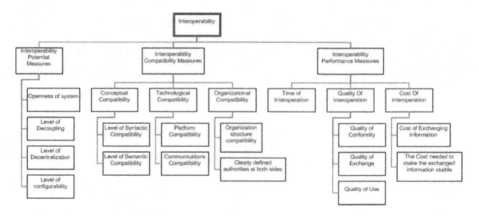

**Fig. 2.** Interoperability Criteria/sub-criteria hierarchy

**Step 2: Identify the enterprise-specific criteria and sub-criteria of interoperability and their level of importance (weight);**

The defined criteria are general for enterprises. In this step, an approach is proposed to specify the weight of interoperability criteria and sub-criteria according to the areas of focus in the enterprise. According to [37] and [38], four main aspects (sub architectures or layers) has been specified for EA, which are Business Architecture layer (BAL), Data Architecture layer (DAL), Software Architecture layer (SAL) and Technology Architecture layer (TAL). There are other classifications such as [39] that define 6 aspects for EA, but here we focus on the first classification.

**Step 2.1: Identify the EA layer each criteria/sub-criteria belongs to;**

As described before, we have specified four main aspects (sub architectures layers) for EA based on [37] and [38], which are Business Architecture layer, Data Architecture layer, Software Architecture layer and technology Architecture layer. In this step an EA expert should specify the EA layer(s) that each criteria/sub-criteria belongs to. One criteria/sub-criteria can belong to more than one EA layer. We have performed this mapping. Table 2 presents the relationship between interoperability criteria/sub-criteria and EA layers.

**Step 2.2: Obtain Individual data about the importance (weight) of each EA Layer in the context of the utility;**

Regarding the fact that the analysis method used in this paper is AHP, weight of EA layers should be assigned by pair-wise comparison. So, a questionnaire is designed which contains a description of interoperability in each EA layer. For this purpose, the most important and tangible criteria of interoperability for each EA layer are described. Then some of the main experts of the enterprise are asked to fill the questionnaire and do pair-wise comparison between the EA layers. They should give a number between 1 and 9 to each comparison between two layers. This number represents the opinion of the expert about the importance of the considered layer compared to the other layer in the context of interoperability in the enterprise. The outcome of this step using AHP, is one vector per participant with relative weights on the importance of each EA layer in the enterprise.

**Table 2.** Interoperability Criteria/sub-criteria and their related EA Layers

| Criteria/Sub-criteria | Related EA Layers |
|---|---|
| Openness of system | All layers |
| Level of Decoupling | BAL, SAL |
| Level of Decentralization | BAL, SAL |
| Level of Configurability | SAL |
| Level of Syntactic Compatibility | DAL, SAL |
| Level of Semantic Compatibility | BAL, DAL, SAL |
| Platform Compatibility | TAL |
| Communications Compatibility | TAL |
| Organization Structure Compatibility | BAL |
| Clearly defined authorities at both sides | BAL |
| Time of Interoperation | BAL, SAL |
| Quality of Conformity | All layers |
| Quality of Exchange | All layers |
| Quality of Use | All layers |
| Cost of Exchanging information | All layers |
| The Cost needed to make the exchanged information usable | All layers |

**Step 2.3: Synthesize data;**

The median value of the individual vectors produced in the previous step, is then used to create a single vector, called PEAL (Prioritized list of EA Layers). This vector represents the weight of each EA layer in the context of interoperability in the enterprise.

**Step 2.4: Specify the weight of each criteria/sub-criteria;**

The weight of each criteria/sub-criteria of interoperability is equal to the weight of the EA layer it belongs to and:

- If a criteria/sub-criteria belongs to more than one EA layer, then its weight will be the maximum weight of the EA layers.
- If the weight of a criteria/sub-criteria is zero, then the criteria/sub-criteria and all its sub-criteria should be omitted

In this approach, the reason of indirectly giving weights to criteria/sub-criteria using the EA layers, instead of directly doing so by the experts, is related to the knowledge of the enterprises' experts. The enterprises' experts might not have enough knowledge about all the criteria/sub-criteria of a quality attribute and by using a more abstract grouping it becomes easier for them to prioritize the criteria/sub-criteria of the quality attribute.

**Step 3: Introduce different EA scenarios (candidates) to be assessed;**

In this step, different EA scenarios to be assessed should be described completely so that participants understand the differences and similarities between them.

**Step 4: Identify which candidate best fits interoperability measures;**
In this step, different EA scenarios are assessed and prioritized using AHP. Through this step, we use the opinion of different EA experts for selecting the best candidate scenario.

### Step 4.1: Obtain individual data about the priority of candidates for each criteria/sub-criteria;

In this sub-step, for each of the leaf nodes in the criteria/sub-criteria hierarchy, EA candidate scenarios are compared with each other using pair-wise comparison process.

As a result of applying AHP, each candidate scenario is assigned a normalized value which represents its priority within all candidate scenarios. The outcome of the prioritization process is one vector per participant with relative weights on the compliance of the EA scenarios with interoperability in the enterprise. We call each resultant vector individual Prioritized list of Candidates (iPC).

### Step 4.2: Synthesize data;

The individual vectors created in the previous section are then synthesized into a combined view of all of the participants. We have found that the easiest way to do this is by taking the median values of all of the participants. This resultant vector is called Prioritized list of Candidates (PC).

**Step 5: Determine the uncertainty in the selection;**
In order to obtain the uncertainty in our selection we need to calculate the variance for each EA scenario candidate i. Since each value in PCQA vector set is the average of k values (each vector set includes the data obtained from each participant and k represents the number of participants), we can calculate the variance of these sets of data in the ordinary way.

The uncertainty in our selection is equal to the variance of PCQA vector sets:

$$\text{Uncertainty for EA scenario candidate } i = 1/k(\sum_{i,j}(iPC_{i,j} - PC_{i,j})^2 \qquad (3)$$

If there is high uncertainty, this may indicate that the architecture candidates and the quality attribute are not so well understood by the participants, and that further investigations are necessary before the final architecture decision is taken.

## 3   A Case Study Using the Method

In order to illustrate the method described in this paper, we present a summary of an experiment conducted using the method. This is done to give a more comprehensive presentation of how the method can be used.

Our case study is conducted in Ports & Maritime Organization of Iran (PMO).

This enterprise as the maritime administration of Iran administers the ports and commercial maritime affairs of the country.

Below, we describe how each step of the method is applied in the study. Because of lack of space, the application of the approach in PMO is described precisely. Note that in the proposed approach for interoperability, step 1 and 2.1 are always the same.

**Step 1: Identify interoperability criteria/sub-criteria;**
As described in section 2.2, Fig. 2 illustrates the criteria/sub-criteria hierarchy of interoperability

**Step 2: Identify the enterprise-specific criteria and sub-criteria of quality attributes and their level of importance (weight);**

**Step 2.1: Identify the EA layer that each criteria/sub-criteria belongs to;**
As described before, Table 2 presents the mapping between interoperability criteria/sub-criteria and EA layers.

**Step 2.2: Obtain Individual data about the importance (weight) of each EA Layer in the context of the utility;**
For this purpose, a questionnaire was designed in which it described interoperability by using the most important and tangible criteria in each EA layer. Then ten domain experts of the enterprise were asked to fill the questionnaire and do pair-wise comparison between the EA layers. At the end of this step, we gathered 10 vectors, as the result of using AHP method, each containing relative weights on the importance of each EA layer in the enterprise.

**Step 2.3: Synthesize data;**
Table 3 illustrates PEAL, which is the median value of the individual vectors produced in the previous step.

**Table 3.** The importance of EA layers as a result of using AHP

| Architecture Layer | Weight |
|---|---|
| Business Architecture Layer | 0.2 |
| Data Architecture Layer | 0.3 |
| Software Architecture Layer | 0.2 |
| Technology Architecture Layer | 0.3 |

**Step 2.4: Specify the weight of each criteria/sub-criteria;**
Table 4 represents the weight of each criteria/sub-criteria of interoperability.

**Step 3: Introduce different EA scenarios (candidates) to be assessed;**
One of the functionalities of PMO is to interoperate with some Maritime Shipping Agencies. These agencies give different maritime and shipping services. PMO issues different certificates for qualified agencies and allows them to provide related services. Also PMO supervises their services and their quality of work. Regarding the fact that interoperability between PMO and these agencies is important for PMO, one criteria for prioritizing these agencies, is their ability to interoperate efficiently with PMO. There are times when PMO wants to prioritize maritime shipping agencies according to their interoperability levels.

Here we consider two maritime shipping agencies and the following step presents the process of prioritizing them.

**Table 4.** Weight of each criteria/sub-criteria of interoperability in PMO

| Criteria/Sub-criteria | Weight |
|---|---|
| Openness of system | 0.3 |
| Level of Decoupling | 0.2 |
| Level of Decentralization | 0.2 |
| Level of Configurability | 0.2 |
| Level of Syntactic Compatibility | 0.3 |
| Level of Semantic Compatibility | 0.3 |
| Platform Compatibility | 0.3 |
| Communications Compatibility | 0.3 |
| Organization Structure Compatibility | 0.2 |
| Clearly defined authorities at both sides | 0.2 |
| Time of Interoperation | 0.2 |
| Quality of Conformity | 0.3 |
| Quality of Exchange | 0.3 |
| Quality of Use | 0.3 |
| Cost of Exchanging information | 0.3 |
| The Cost needed to make the exchanged information usable | 0.3 |

**Step 4: Identify which candidate best fits the interoperability measures;**
In this step, to assess and prioritize the EA scenarios, we used the opinion of five EA experts.

**Step 4.1: Obtain individual data about the priority of candidates for each criteria/sub-criteria;**
The EA experts were asked to compare the EA scenarios based on each of the leaf nodes in the criteria/sub-criteria hierarchy.

The outcome of the prioritization process is one vector per participant with relative weights on the compliance of the EA scenarios with EA interoperability in the enterprise.

**Step 4.2: Synthesize data;**
Table 5 illustrates prioritized list of candidates of PMO for EA interoperability.

**Table 5.** Prioritized list of EA scenarios

| EA Scenario | Weight |
|---|---|
| EA Scenario1 | 0.4 |
| EA Scenario2 | 0.6 |
| Sum | 1 |

**Step 5: Determine the uncertainty in the selection;**
Here we had only two scenarios to choose from, so the VAR vector has identical elements as shown in Table 6:

**Table 6.** The variance of Prioritized list of EA scenarios

| EA Scenario | Variance |
|-------------|----------|
| EA Scenario1 | 0.010776 |
| EA Scenario2 | 0.010776 |

So the uncertainty of our selection is equal to 0.01 which represents that the results are acceptable.

## 4 Conclusion and Future Work

In this paper we present a quantitative assessment method of EA quality attribute achievement for different EA scenarios and use it for interoperability. This method can be applied to indicate the architecture candidates that best suit the interoperability criteria defined by the enterprise. It also can be used to hold focused discussions on areas where there are disagreements, between participants of the assessment, to increase the confidence that the correct decision is taken.

This paper is a customization of the idea of [40] in the field of interoperability.

The major benefits of the method are listed as below:

- It considers enterprises' situation in specifying and giving weight to different criteria/sub-criteria of the quality attributes
- It considers all possible combinations in assessing a quality attribute
- It calculates consistency ratio of each AHP prioritization and also uncertainty of the final selection. If these values are out of specified range, the corresponding process should be redone with more precise information or by other participants with more experience.
- It uses the experience and knowledge of EA experts and domain experts and clearly indicates disagreements between participants.

As future work we can consider case studies covering other quality attributes besides interoperability and illustrate the tradeoff between them supported by the approach. As another future work, we can introduce the use of Analytical Network Process (ANP) as another MCDM method in EA Analysis. This method considers the interdependencies between hierarchy nodes and creates a network of nodes. This contradicts with AHP that considers each node independently.

## References

1. Nightingale, D.J., Rhodes, D.H.: Enterprise Systems Architecting: Emerging Art and Science within Engineering Systems. In: MIT Engineering Systems Symposium (2004)
2. Armour, F.J., Kaisler, S.H., Liu, S.Y.: Building an enterprise architecture step by step. IEEE IT Professional 1(4), 31–39 (1999)
3. Bass, L., Klein, M., Bachmann, F.: Quality Attribute Design Primitives and the Attribute Driven Design Method. In: 4th International Workshop on Product Family Engineering (2001)

4. Chen, D., Vallespir, B., Daclin, N.: An Approach for Enterprise Interoperability Measurement. In: Proceedings of MoDISE-EUS (2008)
5. IEEE, IEEE (Institute of Electrical and Electronics Engineers): Standard Computer Dictionary- A Compilation of IEEE Standard Computer Glossaries (1990)
6. WordNet Browser 2.1, Princeton University Cognitive Science Lab
7. ISO 14258, Concepts and Rules for Enterprise Models TC 184/SC5/WG1 (1998)
8. ATHENA Integrated Project, Guidelines and Best Practices for Applying the ATHENA Interoperability Framework to Support SME Participation in Digital Ecosystems, Deliverable DA8.2 (2007)
9. EIF, European Interoperability Framework for PAN-European EGovernment services, IDA working document - Version 4.2 (2004)
10. INTEROP, Enterprise Interoperability-Framework and knowledge corpus - Final report, INTEROP NoE, FP6 – Contract n° 508011, Deliverable DI.3 (May 21, 2007)
11. Kazman, R., Abowd, G., Bass, L., Clements, P.: Scenario-Based Analysis of Software Architecture. IEEE Software, 47–55 (1996)
12. Clements, P., Kazman, R., Klein, M.: Evaluating Software Architectures: Methods and Case Studies. Addison-Wesley, Reading (2001)
13. Gacek, C.: Detecting Architectural Mismatch During System Composition. PhD. Thesis, University of Southern California (1998)
14. Allen, R., Douence, R., Garlan, D.: Specifying and Analyzing Dynamic Software Architectures. In: Proceedings of the 1998 Conference on Fundamental Approaches to Software Engineering (1998)
15. Medvidovic, N., Rosenblum, D., Taylor, R.: A Language and Environment for Architecture-Based Software Development and Evolution. In: Proceedings of the 21st International Conference on Software Engineering (1999)
16. Svahnberg, M., Wohlin, C., Lundberg, L., Mattsson, M.: A quality-driven decision-support method for identifying software architecture candidates. International Journal of Software Engineering and Knowledge Engineering 13(5), 547–573 (2003)
17. Al-Naeem, T., Gorton, I., Babar, M.A., Rabhi, F., Benatallah, B.: A quality-driven systematic approach for architecting distributed software applications. In: Proceedings of the 27th International Conference on Software Engineering (ICSE), St. Louis, USA, pp. 244–253 (2005)
18. Svahnberg, M., Wohlin, C., Lundberg, L., Mattsson, M.: A method for understanding quality attributes in software architecture structures. In: Proceedings of the 14th international conference on Software engineering and knowledge engineering (SEKE), pp. 819–826 (2002)
19. Davidsson, P., Johansson, S., Svahnberg, M.: Using the Analytic Hierarchy Process for Evaluating Multi-Agent System Architecture Candidates. In: 6th International Workshop on Agent-Oriented Software Engineering (AOSE), pp. 205–217 (2005)
20. Buyukozkan, G., Ruan, D.: Evaluation of software development projects using a fuzzy multi-criteria decision approach. Mathematics and Computers in Simulation 77(5-6), 464–475 (2008)
21. Mikhailov, L., Tsvetinov, P.: Evaluation of services using a fuzzy analytic hierarchy process. Appl. Soft Comput. 5, 23–33 (2004)
22. Lee, K., Choi, H., Lee, D., Kang, S.: Quantitative Measurement of Quality Attribute Preferences Using Conjoint Analysis. In: Gilroy, S.W., Harrison, M.D. (eds.) DSV-IS 2005. LNCS, vol. 3941, pp. 213–224. Springer, Heidelberg (2006)

23. Zhu, L., Aurum, A., Gorton, I., Jeffery, D.: Tradeoff and Sensitivity Analysis in Software Architecture Evaluation Using Analytic Hierarchy Process. Software Quality Journal 13(4), 357–375 (2005)
24. Reddy, A., Naidu, M., Govindarajulu, P.: An Integrated approach of Analytical Hierarchy Process Model and Goal Model (AHP-GP Model) for Selection of Software Architecture. International journal of Computer Science and Network Security 7(10), 108–117 (2007)
25. Johnson, P., Lagerström, R., Närman, P., Simonsson, M.: Enterprise architecture analysis with extended influence diagrams. Information Systems Frontiers 9(2-3), 163–180 (2007)
26. Närman, P., Johnson, P., Nordström, L.: Enterprise Architecture: A Framework Supporting System Quality Analysis. In: 11th IEEE Enterprise Distributed Object Computing Conference, pp. 130–141 (2007)
27. Johnson, P., Lagerström, R., Närman, P., Simonsson, M.: Extended Influence Diagrams for Enterprise Architecture Analysis. In: 10th IEEE Enterprise Distributed Object Computing Conference, pp. 3–12 (2006)
28. Johnson, P., Lagerström, R., Närman, P., Simonsson, M.: Extended Influence Diagrams for System Quality Analysis. Journal Of Software (JSW) 2(3), 30–42 (2007)
29. Lagerström, R.: Analyzing System Maintainability Using Enterprise Architecture Models. In: Proceedings of the 2nd Workshop on Trends in Enterprise Architecture Research (TEAR 2007), St Gallen, Switzerland, pp. 31–39 (2007)
30. Johnson, P., Johansson, E., Sommestad, T., Ullberg, J.: A Tool for Enterprise Architecture Analysis. In: 11th IEEE Enterprise Distributed Object Computing Conference, pp. 142–156 (2007)
31. Lagerström, R., Johnson, P.: Using Architectural Models to Predict the Maintainability of Enterprise Systems. In: 12th European Conference on Software Maintenance and Reengineering, pp. 248–252 (2008)
32. Ullberg, J., Lagerström, R., Johnson, P.: Johnson P.: Enterprise Architecture: A Service Interoperability Analysis Framework. In: Proceedings of the 4th International Interoperability for Enterprise Software and Applications Conference (I-ESA 2008), pp. 611–623. Springer, Berlin (2008)
33. Karlsson, J., Wohlin, C., Regnell, B.: An Evaluation of Methods for Prioritizing Software Requirements. Information and Software Technology 39(14-15), 938–947 (1998)
34. Saaty, T.L.: The Analytic Hierarchy Process. McGraw Hill, Inc., New York (1980)
35. Saaty, T.L., Vargas, L.G.: Models, Methods, Concepts &Applications of the Analytic Hierarchy Process. Kluwer Academic Publishers, Dordrecht (2001)
36. Buyukyazici, M., Sucu, M.: The Analytic Hierarchy and Analytic Network Processes. Hacettepe Journal of Mathematics and Statistics 32, 65–73 (2003)
37. Federal Chief Information Officer (CIO) Council: Federal Enterprise Architecture Framework (FEAF). Version 1.1 (1999)
38. Spewak, S.H.: Enterprise Architecture Planning, Developing a Blueprint for Data, Applications and Technology. John Wiley & Sons, Inc., Chichester (1992)
39. Sowa, J.F., Zachman, J.A.: Extending and Formalizing the Framework for Information Systems Architecture. IBM Journal 31(3), 914–945 (1992) IBM Publication G321-5488. 914-945-3836
40. Razavi, M., Shams Aliee, F.: A New AHP-based Approach towards Enterprise Architecture Quality Attribute Analysis. In: Proceedings of the IEEE International conference on Research Challenges in Information Science, pp. 333–342 (2009)

# Classifying Enterprise Architecture Analysis Approaches

Sabine Buckl, Florian Matthes, and Christian M. Schweda

Chair for Software Engineering of Business Information Systems (sebis),
Technische Universität München,
Boltzmannstr. 3, 85748 Garching, Germany
{buckls,schweda}@in.tum.de
http://wwwmatthes.in.tum.de

**Abstract.** Enterprise architecture (EA) management forms a commonly accepted means to enhance the alignment of business and IT, and to support the managed evolution of the enterprise. One major challenge of EA management is to provide decision support by analyzing as-is states of the architecture as well as assessing planned future states. Thus, different kinds of analysis regarding the EA exist, each relying on certain conditions and demands for models, methods, and techniques.

In this paper we present a classification schema for EA analysis approaches to examine this topic. The classification schema is used to investigate the state-of-the-art of EA analysis by characterizing existing approaches according to the presented dimensions. Based on the results of this classification, future areas of research regarding EA analysis are derived.

**Keywords:** Enterprise architecture management, EA analysis, ex ante/ex post analysis, behavioral/structural analysis, EA analysis classification.

## 1 Introduction and Motivation

In large enterprises, the application landscape, as the entirety of the employed business applications [1], is an important asset, which forms both a critical support factor for business and a costly investment constantly demanding maintenance operations. Consequently, managing the application landscape has not only recently become a challenge, today's enterprises have to address. The management of the application landscape is not an isolated task but a far-reaching endeavor, which has to be undertaken embedded in the context of enterprise architecture (EA) management. The holistic perspective of EA management sets up a framework for application landscape management, broadening the focus to related parts of the enterprise, such as business or infrastructure aspects (see Figure 1). These related parts of the overall architecture of the enterprise are themselves subject to other well-established management processes – the so called enterprise-level management processes, e.g. project portfolio management, strategies and goals management, and IT architecture management [2]. By linking these processes, to which application landscape management also belongs,

R. Poler, M. van Sinderen, and R. Sanchis (Eds.): IWEI 2009, LNBIP 38, pp. 66–79, 2009.

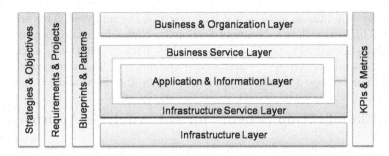

**Fig. 1.** Layers and crossfunctions of a holistic EA management approach [3]

to the EA management process, the overall alignment of business and IT in an enterprise can be fostered.

In the light of the increased interest from practitioners, different approaches to EA management have been developed in academic research [4,5,6,7], by practitioners [8,9,10,11], standardization bodies [12,13], and tool vendors [3]. These approaches provide frameworks, methods, and tools to facilitate EA management endeavors, but as of today they focus on *structural* aspects of the EA or of parts thereof, such as dependencies between business processes and business applications. Based on analyses of these aspects, decisions about the future of the EA are made and plans for a *managed evolution* (cf. [14]) are created. Currently, the dynamic behavior of the enterprise system[1] is not considered nor analyzed, although wrong decisions and inappropriate plans on the one hand might lead to high and long-term consequential costs, and on the other hand may have unforeseen impacts on the behavior of the highly dynamic system. The behavior is usually far more complex than the topological structure of the system is likely to indicate. The term *dynamic complexity*, which points to this fact, is a widely known and accepted in many management disciplines. First references date back to the $60^{ths}$ of the last century (cf. the *Forrester effect* [16]).

The dynamic complexity arising from the behavior of and interactions between the entities, which are considered to make up the EA, has yet not been an important topic in EA management research. This is especially surprising, as in some bordering areas many discussions on dynamic complexity have been undertaken, e.g. in the research of Ultra-Large-Scale Systems [17]. Even more prominent are the discussions in the area of business process management, where also techniques and methods for analyzing and evaluating dynamic complexity were developed (see e.g. [18,19]).

Dynamic complexity in the enterprise system seems to us as a promising field of activity in EA management research, where the focus of the techniques for *EA analysis* can be extended. As a guidance for further research, we develop a classification schema for EA analysis, which considers the different types of

---

[1] We use the term *enterprise system* to emphasize on the systems nature of an enterprise that is itself a system, which consists of systems, and is surrounded by systems [15].

complexity but also aspects as e.g. the reach of the analyses. This schema is presented in Section 2. In subsequent Section 3, we classify existing approaches to EA analysis according to the dimensions of the schema. From there, we elaborate on the omissions in current research and shape different lines of activity to close the experienced gap. These ideas are presented in final Section 4.

## 2    A Classification Schema for EA Analysis Approaches

In the last years, quite a few scientific publications bearing the term *EA analysis* in their title have been published. Before discussing selected prominent approaches in the following, we should mention that albeit the increased popularity, no common definition of the term *EA analysis* has yet emerged. This may be caused by the plurality of techniques and methods that are subsumed under the term. Additionally, the approaches differ in respect to their coverage of the EA. To advance the development of this area, we do not try to give a comprehensive definition of the term, but present a classification schema (see Table 1) for analysis approaches. The dimensions of classification introduced therein, are explain below.

**Table 1.** Classification schema for EA analysis approaches

| Body of Analysis | structure | behavior statistics | dynamic behavior |
|---|---|---|---|
| Time Reference | ex-post | | ex-ante |
| Analysis Technique | expert-based | rule-based | indicator-based |
| Analysis Concern | functional | | non-functional |
| Self-Referentiality | none | single-level | multi-level |

**Body of Analysis: Structure, behavior statistics,** and **dynamic behavior**
As discussed in Section 1, enterprises are complex systems, which encompass a dense web of interconnections. Together with the sheer number of constituents, this number of interconnections contributes to the *structural complexity* of the enterprise system, reflected in the corresponding EA models. EA analyses have to deal with this complexity by e.g. providing mechanisms to aggregate concepts to a higher level of abstraction or to overleap concepts in transitive relationships. Aside the complex structure, the enterprise system's constituents exert a *complex behavior*, which also forms a valuable object for analyses. In particular, statistic information about the system's behavior may be highly relevant to the stakeholders of EA management. Such analyses present behavioral aspects in an aggregated manner, e.g. as *moving-average* of a certain behavioral attribute. This statistic information provides an aggregation of lower level information concerned with the dynamic behavior of the system's constituents, i.e. the time-series of values of an attribute or a stream of discrete events. The *dynamic behavior* is especially an interesting object of analysis, if *pathological* effects in the behavior are considered, e.g. the impact of a system failure propagating over time.

## Time Reference: **Ex-post** and **ex-ante**

EA analyses are performed on models of the architecture. Regarding these architectural models, two types can be distinguished: models of *current architectures* and of *planned architectures*. Models of the first type describe the architecture of an existing, i.e. implemented EA, while models of the second type mainly refer to planning scenarios for the architecture. In this respect, analyses have to act differently on the two types of models – in the case with current architectures, both information on the structure and the behavior is available, i.e. can be measured[2]. In contrast, architectural plans describe the planned structure, where information on the resulting behavior is not present, as the architecture scenario is neither implemented nor operated. But not only for the question of behavior the distinction between *ex-post* analyses, i.e. ones targeting current architectures, and *ex-ante* analyses on planned architectures is sensible. The same is true for analyses on the structure, which is fixed for current architectures, while architectural scenarios are inevitably connected to a higher level of uncertainty. They hence have at least a partially predictive character. The aforementioned facts motivate the distinction concerning the point in time(*ex-post* and *ex-ante*).

## Analysis Technique: **Expert-based**, **rule-based**, and **indicator-based**

EA analyses can employ different levels of formalization ranging from informal expert-based techniques to formal indicator-based ones. The *expert-based* approaches are the most flexible but also most time-consuming ones, and depend on the experience and expertise of the executing person. Therein, one or more EA experts analyze properties of the EA along appropriate architecture views, as e.g. reports or graphical visualizations. Such analyses may produce results that range from rather concrete advices to more general and abstract ideas for future architecture development. *Rule-based* analyses are performed at an increased level of formalization and can consistently be automated. Thereby, rules describe certain architectural constellations, which are either desirable or should be avoided, i.e. they can represent *patterns* or *anti-patterns* for an EA. An even higher level of formalization is reached by *indicator-based* analysis techniques. Where rule-based techniques can only assess the absence or presence of certain architectural patterns, indicators can be used to quantitatively assess architectural properties, as e.g. complexity. Commonly, the values of these indicators are derived from the values of observable architecture properties by computation. While producing the most expressive and most directly interpretable analysis results, indicator-based techniques are narrow in their focus and their results have to be interpreted carefully. In particular, the analysts must keep in mind, that an indicator is always based on assumptions on the architecture, who – if not longer valid – deprive the indicator of its expressive power.

## Analysis Concern: **Functional** and **non-functional**

Enterprises are designed towards performing enterprise functions, such as production or sales. Thereby, we can assume that an EA is developed with certain

---

[2] Nevertheless, the information might not be collected due to complexity or cost reasons.

*functional* requirements in mind. With the help of EA analysis, the fulfillment of these requirements by the enterprise system, expressed in its architecture, can be assessed. In contrast, the enterprise system also has *non-functional* properties, as e.g. execution times or throughput. These properties might also be interesting for analysis, especially in cases, where the fulfillment of the functional requirements is given and alternatives for achieving this fulfillment should be compared. Some EA management practitioners mention *economic concerns* [11], as e.g. operating or maintenance costs, and want those to be analyzed especially for EA planning. We nevertheless do not further distinguish between non-functional and economic concerns, as we regard the latter to be a specialization of the former. The distinction between functional and non-functional concerns resembles the similar distinction as discussed in the discipline of software engineering, where also different analysis approaches exist targeting both types of aspects (cf. e.g. [20]). For the context of the EA, this distinction is also undertaken in [21], where *functional* and *quantitative* analyses are juxtaposed. We argue that the terms functional and non-functional are more appropriate, as *quantative* alludes to a certain type of analysis result, but does not make prescriptions on the analyzed concern. Put in other words, a non-functional requirement as e.g. security could be analyzed in a non-quantative way.

**Consideration of Self-Referentiality: None, Single-level, and Multi-level**
As shown in Figure 1, organizational structures as well as strategic planning concepts are also considered to be part of the EA. In this vein, the element of *self-referentiality* is introduced into the field of EA management in general and EA analysis in special. In particular, the groups and roles in the enterprise actually performing the EA analysis can also be modeled in the corresponding EA model. The situation can become even more complex, as the activities for managing, describing, and planning the EA can be managed, described, and planned as parts of an EA. This agrees with the interpretation of the enterprise as a *living system* having the property of *autopoiesis*. Such system is in accordance to [22] defined as:

> a [system] organized as a network of processes of production, transformation and destruction of components which:
> **(i)** through their interactions and transformations continuously regenerate and realize the network of processes (relations) that produced them, and
> **(ii)** constitute it [the system] as a concrete unity in space in which they (the components) exist by specifying the topological domain of its realization as such a network.

Regarding this self-creating and -updating characteristics of the EA, an approach to EA analysis has to decide, to which extent these higher-level interactions are considered. In a simple model, the architectural aspects behind the activities of EA management are not considered, i.e. there is no consideration of self-referentiality. A more elaborate analysis model would include one level of self-referentiality, i.e. it would analyze the EA management activities as EA constituents. A multi-level approach goes even further and considers the activities of the meta-processes of EA management (such as *EA management governance*, cf. [23]) to be part of the EA model. Introducing EA related activities into the EA itself is very likely to increase the complexity of the corresponding analyses, but may simplify the understanding of *emergent* behavior [24] in the enterprise system.

In [21] another *analysis dimension* is presented, distinguishing between *analytical* and *simulation* analysis techniques. Thereby, simulation-based analysis techniques are understood as *executing a model* for performing the analysis, while analytical techniques aim at finding a closed solution for an analysis model. In contrast, we do not estimate the importance of that distinction high enough to be beneficial for our subsequent classification.

# 3   State-of-the-Art in Enterprise Architecture Analysis

Based on the classification schema introduced in preceding Section 2, in the following the state-of-the-art in EA analysis is investigated. In particular, prominent approaches to this field are introduced and revisited in respect to the classification dimensions of the schema.

In [25], an approach to perform EA analysis with XML is presented. The article hence puts a strong emphasis on issue how to represent the EA in a model for performing analyses. This model is rather fine grained, proposing to use *state-machines* to include behavioral descriptions as well as XML elements to represent structural information about the architecture. The time reference in the analyses is not explicitly alluded to, although the structural analyses can be applied both ex-ante and ex-post, while the state-machine based modeling of EA behavior points towards an ex-ante analysis of behavioral aspects. The question how to calibrate behavior models against measured behavior is nevertheless not discussed in the article. Also, the question of the employed analysis technique is not detailed, but indications pointing towards rule-based analysis techniques exist. When it comes to the possible analysis concerns, the paper does neither advocate functional nor non-functional properties of the EA. The approach presented nevertheless can be regarded generic enough to support both types of concerns. Self-referentiality of EA analysis and management is not discussed in the article. This leads to a classification of the approach as shown in Table 2.

A more quantitative approach to EA analysis is proposed in [26], where exemplary indicators for analyzing EA behavior are provided. These indicators are

**Table 2.** Classification of EA analysis approach of [25]

| Body of Analysis | structure | | | dynamic behavior |
|---|---|---|---|---|
| Time Reference | ex-post | | | (ex-ante) |
| Analysis Technique | | rule-based | | |
| Analysis Concern | (functional) | | (non-functional) | |
| Self-Referentiality | none | | | |

developed to provide aggregated information on the behavior of certain EA artifacts, i.e. to compute behavior statistics. The analysis model presented in the approach integrates into the ArchiMate architecture description language[3], whose concepts are augmented with additional properties reflecting non-functional aspects of the EA, as e.g. the execution or completion time for a business process. The time reference in the analysis is discussed alongside the question of the quantitative input for the analysis model. In particular, the authors highlight that measuring the behavior of an existing system can provide valuable input, but also rise the question of reproducible circumstances for the measurements. For systems, which are still to be developed, estimates for properties, e.g. based on comparable architectures, are noted as possible source for quantitative information. Based on this information, performance measures for the (planned) system are derived analytically, i.e. the values for descriptive indicators are computed. The question of self-referentiality of EA analysis and management is not alluded to in the article, whose approach can be classified as shown in Table 3.

**Table 3.** Classification of EA analysis approach of [26]

| Body of Analysis | | behavior statistics | |
|---|---|---|---|
| Time Reference | ex-post | | ex-ante |
| Analysis Technique | | | indicator-based |
| Analysis Concern | | | non-functional |
| Self-Referentiality | none | | |

Two prominent approaches for EA analysis are presented in [27] and [28], respectively. These approaches vary significantly concerning their origins and concerning the concepts, which they employ. Concerning the classification schema, both approaches are nevertheless quite similar and fit into one classification as shown in Table 4. The two approaches support both ex-ante and ex-post analyses of enterprise systems represented in EA models. In particular, [27] emphasizes the importance of an indicator system, which is used for analyses there, as means to support communication in an enterprise. The focus of both approaches lies on statistic information arising from the behavior of the enterprise system, although to a limited amount also structural aspects of the EA are analyzed. Beside the indicator-based analysis technique, a prominent difference exists: the approach of [28] aims at the development of single indicators, while [27] goes even further. In particular, the latter approach seeks to develop integrated and consistent indicator systems. Regarding the analysis concern, both approaches focus on non-functional requirements, with the approach of [27] centering on more economic indicators, whereas [28] puts an emphasis on *classical* non-functional aspects, such as availability. Finally, it can be said that the approaches restrict themselves to analyses of the EA; the self-referential character of EA management is hence not considered.

---

[3] For more information see http://archimate.telin.nl

**Table 4.** Classification of EA analysis approaches of [27] and [28]

| Body of Analysis | (structure) | behavior statistics | |
|---|---|---|---|
| Time Reference | ex-post | | ex-ante |
| Analysis Technique | | | indicator-based |
| Analysis Concern | | | non-functional |
| Self-Referentiality | none | | |

The topic of EA analysis is also discussed in [11]. There an emphasis is put on the utilization of EA models, which have been created during other EA management activities. These models reflect structural aspects of the EA, thus limiting the body of analysis on such aspects. Furthermore, existing enterprise systems reflected in their EAs are analyzed according to different concerns. The majority of these concerns is functional, e.g. homogeneity of the application landscape or the interdependencies between the business applications are considered. Complementing, two economic concerns, namely *costs* and *benefits*, are alluded to as typical EA analysis concerns. Nevertheless, the measures for those costs and benefits remain on a rather abstract level. The different analysis concerns are addressed by different techniques, of which the majority is expert-based, i.e. they utilize specific viewpoints to present architecture information to an enterprise architect, who informally assesses e.g. the level of homogeneity. When it comes to the economic concerns, the predominance of the expert-based analysis is broken in favor of a few quantitative indicators, which are especially used to operationalize benefits. All the different types of analysis as proposed in [11] target the enterprise system as reflected in its EA – the corresponding management system is not discussed in the analyses. This leads to a classification as shown in Table 5.

**Table 5.** Classification of EA analysis approach of [11]

| Body of Analysis | structure | | |
|---|---|---|---|
| Time Reference | ex-post | | |
| Analysis Technique | expert-based | | (indicator-based) |
| Analysis Concern | functional | | (non-functional) |
| Self-Referentiality | none | | |

Agreeing with the overall understanding of EA analysis as proposed in [11] and discussed in [29], a dedicated support of *impact analyses* is shown in [30]. In particular, the EA is thereby understood as a directed graph reflecting the structure of the enterprise system. On this graph, rule-based analyses are performed to assess and evaluate the transitive impact of an EA constituent, e.g. in cases of failure. Thereby, the analyses are applied to current architectures, although the proposed method is not limited in this respect and could hence also be applied on planned architectures. Regarding the analysis concerns, the approach does not make assumptions, i.e. it can handle both functional and non-functional ones. The following two analysis questions taken from [30] exemplify this: *Which business applications are used during the creation of a selected product?* and *Which applications fail, if a certain server fails?*. Due to its high generality, the approach would not be restricted to pure EA analyses, but could also employ higher level processes and concepts. Nevertheless, the paper does not account for this method but limits the approach to structural analyses of the enterprise system. This leads to a classification as shown in Table 6.

**Table 6.** Classification of EA analysis approach of [30]

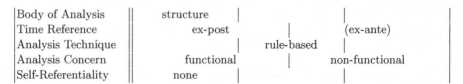

| Body of Analysis | structure | | | |
|---|---|---|---|---|
| Time Reference | ex-post | | (ex-ante) | |
| Analysis Technique | | rule-based | | |
| Analysis Concern | functional | | non-functional | |
| Self-Referentiality | none | | | |

Quite different from the aforementioned analysis approaches is the approach presented in [31], which centers around the idea of *intentional modeling*. Based on this idea, not only the EA as the architecture of the enterprise system, but also the architecture behind the EA management processes is analyzed. This especially applies to the process of constructing an EA model, whose motivation and stakeholders are heavily considered. To foster the analyses, intentional modeling concepts from the *i\* language* (cf. [32]) are linked to structural concepts of the EA, such as (business) processes. The models used therein are models of future EAs (and their related EA management processes), which are developed from current architecture models that were annotated with intentional meta-information. The actual analyses are performed by EA experts, as they can account for the different kinds of goals from the intentional models. Especially the so called *soft-goals* demand expert analysis, as they are not easily operationalized. So expert interviews are strongly alluded to as a suitable analysis technique. In most cases, functional properties of the enterprise system are considered during the analyses, although viability analysis (cf. e.g. [33]) further allows to include non-functional factors, as performance or security into the analysis. The classification of the approach according to the schema from Section 2 reads as shown in Table 7.

**Table 7.** Classification of EA analysis approach of [31]

| Body of Analysis | structure | | | |
|---|---|---|---|---|
| Time Reference | | | ex-ante | |
| Analysis Technique | expert-based | | | |
| Analysis Concern | functional | | (non-functional) | |
| Self-Referentiality | | single-level | | |

Summarizing the above classifications of the selected EA analysis approaches, we can show a classification schema referencing the corresponding approaches for the different characteristics in the dimensions of classification. This schema is shown in table 8 to prepare the subsequent discussions on the state-of-the-art in EA analysis in the subsequent section.

**Table 8.** Summarizing classification of the EA analysis approaches

| Body of Analysis | structure [11],[25],([27],[28]) [30],[31] | behavior statistics [26],[27],[28] | dynamic behavior [25] |
|---|---|---|---|
| Time Reference | ex-post [11],[25],[26],[27],[28],[30] | ex-ante ([25]),[26],[27],[28],([30]),[31] | |
| Analysis Technique | expert-based [11],[31] | rule-based [25],[30] | indicator-based ([11]),[26],[27],[28] |
| Analysis Concern | functional [11],([25]),[30],[31] | non-functional ([11],[25]),[26],[27], [28],[30],([31]) | |
| Self-Referentiality | none [11],[25],[26],[27], [28],[30] | single-level model [31] | multi-level model |

# 4  Conclusion and Outlook

In this paper, we presented a classification schema for EA analysis approaches and applied this schema to the state-of-the-art in the field. Thereby, we could show that the different characteristics for almost every dimension of classification are incorporated into at least one approach. The sole exception to this finding is *multi-level* self-referentiality, which actually is not easy to implement, especially as EA management is a relatively new discipline without well-established meta-processes (cf. also [23]). Aside this apparent lack of a supporting approach for meta-EA management analyses, an interesting property can be discovered by considering the overall coverage reached by the different approaches. Subsequently, we discuss this on the different dimensions of classification:

**Body of Analysis:** Predominantly, structural aspects of the EA such as interconnections, are analyzed. This might indebt to the fact, that behavioral information is less frequently collected and mostly used in an aggregated form, i.e. as behavior statistics. Analyzing the dynamics in behavior, e.g. pathological effects, is only discussed in the approach of [25], although the description of the actual analysis method remains vague there. Furthermore, dynamic behavior and behavior statistics are not considered in combination by one of the approaches. We nevertheless see that these bodies of analysis are intrinsically linked to each other.

**Time Reference:** Many approaches analyzed are not specifically designed towards ex-ante or ex-post analyses only, but can be applied in both time references equally. This is not surprising, as most of the approaches focus on structural aspects, which can be handled irrespective of their planning character. When the question comes to approaches analyzing aggregated enterprise behavior, the situation presents itself a bit more complicated. Most likely, the corresponding approaches support ex-post and ex-ante analyses, but refer to the latter only in a side-note, reading like the following: *for applying the technique on planned architectures, estimations have to be made.* The question, how architectural properties for future EAs can be estimated is hence not alluded to in detail in the majority of of the approaches.

**Analysis Technique:** The three characteristics of this dimension are well-applied in the different analysis approaches. On the one hand, this might be caused by the fact that a clear distinction between expert-based analyses and the other characteristics is not always possible based on the approaches' descriptions. When it comes to rule-based and indicator-based, the situation is somewhat different. The approaches are either rule- or indicator-based, but none of them combines both analysis techniques.

**Analysis Concern:** Non-functional and especially economic aspects of the enterprise system are clearly more in the focus of EA analysis approaches, although especially some highly generic approaches are applicable on both types of concerns. Nevertheless, these approaches are most likely to apply the expert-based analysis technique. This might ascribe to the fact that describing the function of an EA constituent is not that easy to perform and hence more structured analysis techniques are hard to apply.

**Self-Referentiality:** Only one of the considered approaches goes beyond a pure EA analysis by also considering the complementing EA management process. This might have manifold reasons aside the aforementioned novelty of the discipline. To name just another important reason, it has to be noted that neither a commonly accepted definition of the EA management function yet exists nor a reference process, one could evaluate the EA management against. This relates the question of self-referentiality in EA analysis approaches to the new and emerging field of EA maturity models (see e.g. [34]), which is under heavy development for a couple of years now.

Concluding it can be said, that the field of EA analysis shows all signs of an emerging discipline. Quite a few approaches to the field exist, differing in origin, technique, and coverage. But as of today, these approaches are not well-linked to each other, as they e.g. employ many different modeling techniques. Advancing the field of EA analysis would hence clearly mean, bringing together the different approaches especially concerning the dimensions *body of analysis*, *time reference*, and *analysis technique*. In particular, the first two dimensions are closely related in this respect – linking dynamic behavior models with behavior statistics models could advance the development of ex-ante analysis. The dynamic models would allow simulation of behavior of planned architectures, thus replacing the vague guessing of estimates, which is widely alluded to. From these dynamic models, behavior statistics could be derived analytically or by simulation. Thereby, the experienced gap in these dimensions could be closed.

In respect to the analysis techniques, a similar argument applies. Certain architecture properties, most likely structural ones, can be easily assessed by rule-based techniques. With the help of these techniques architectural anti-patterns could be matched, ruling out certain planned architectures in advance. After this, more detailed indicator-based analysis techniques could be applied to predict non-functional properties of the planned EA. Thereby, an integrated analysis approach would be provided, allowing to narrow the *search space* by ruling out some options before potentially applying extensive and time-consuming simulation techniques.

Above discussions outline a line of action for future research, in which the somewhat isolated EA analysis approaches are integrated into a conceptual framework. We regard the classification schema as presented in Section 2 to give quite a few indications on how such a framework could be structured. Nevertheless, some challenges are await on the way towards an integrated analysis approach. In particular, we expect the question of a conceptual modeling language for supporting arbitrary EA analyses an interesting one. This would especially be true, if such language was designed to not burden the related EA management activities, as EA documentation or EA planning, with formal mechanisms that are solely needed for EA analyses.

# References

1. Wittenburg, A.: Softwarekartographie: Modelle und Methoden zur systematischen Visualisierung von Anwendungslandschaften. PhD thesis, Fakultät für Informatik, Technische Universität München (2007)
2. Wittenburg, A., Matthes, F., Fischer, F., Hallermeier, T.: Building an integrated it governance platform at the bmw group. International Journal Business Process Integration and Management 2(4) (2007)
3. Matthes, F., Buckl, S., Leitel, J., Schweda, C.M.: Enterprise Architecture Management Tool Survey 2008. Chair for Informatics 19 (sebis), Technische Universität München, Munich (2008)
4. Buckl, S., Ernst, A.M., Lankes, J., Matthes, F.: Enterprise Architecture Management Pattern Catalog (Version 1.0, February 2008). Technical report, Chair for Informatics 19 (sebis), Technische Universität München, Munich, Germany (2008)
5. Fischer, R., Aier, S., Winter, R.: A federated approach to enterprise architecture model maintenance. In: Enterprise Modelling and Information Systems Architectures - Concepts and Applications, Proceedings of the 2nd International Workshop on Enterprise Modelling and Information Systems Architectures (EMISA 2007), St. Goar, Germany, October 8-9, pp. 9–22 (2007)
6. Frank, U.: Multi-perspective enterprise modeling (memo) – conceptual framework and modeling languages. In: Proceedings of the 35th Annual Hawaii International Conference on System Sciences (HICSS 3003), pp. 1258–1267 (2002)
7. Lankhorst, M.: Enterprise Architecture at Work: Modelling, Communication and Analysis. Springer, Heidelberg (2005)
8. Dern, G.: Management von IT-Architekturen (Edition CIO). Vieweg, Wiesbaden (2006)

9. Engels, G., Hess, A., Humm, B., Juwig, O., Lohmann, M., Richter, J.P.: Quasar Enterprise – Anwendungslandschaften serviceorientiert gestalten. dpunkt.verlag, Heidelberg (2008)
10. Keller, W.: IT-Unternehmensarchitektur. dpunkt.verlag, Heidelberg (2007)
11. Niemann, K.D.: From Enterprise Architecture to IT Governance – Elements of Effective IT Management. Vieweg+Teubner, Wiesbaden (2006)
12. van der Torre, L.W.N., Lankhorst, M.M., ter Doest, H.W.L., Campschroer, J.T.P., Arbab, F.: Landscape maps for enterprise architectures. In: Dubois, E., Pohl, K. (eds.) CAiSE 2006. LNCS, vol. 4001, pp. 351–366. Springer, Heidelberg (2006)
13. Department of Defense (DoD) USA: DoD Architecture Framework Version 1.5: Volume I: Definitions and Guidelines (2007), http://www.defenselink.mil/cio-nii/docs/DoDAF_Volume_I.pdf (cited 2009-06-30)
14. Murer, S., Worms, C., Furrer, F.: Managed evolution. Informatik Spektrum 31(6), 527–536 (2008)
15. Harmon, K.: The "systems" nature of enterprise architecture. In: IEEE International Conference on Systems, Man and Cybernetics 2005, pp. 78–58 (2005)
16. Forrest, J.W.: Industrial Dynamics. MIT Press, Cambridge (1961)
17. Pollak, B.: Ultra-Large-Scale Systems – The Software Challenge of the Future. Carnegie Mellon University, Software Engineering Institute, Pittsburgh, USA (2006)
18. Jansen-Vullers, M., Netjes, M.: Business process simulation – a tool survey. In: Seventh Workshop and Tutorial on Practical Use of Coloured Petri Nets and the CPN Tools, Denmark (2006)
19. Laguna, M., Marklund, J.: Business Process Modeling, Simulation, and Design. Prentice Hall PTR, Indianapolis (2004)
20. Sommerville, I.: Software Engineering, 6th edn. Pearson Studium, Munich (2001)
21. Lankhorst, M.: Introduction to enterprise architecture. In: Enterprise Architecture at Work. Springer, Heidelberg (2005)
22. Varela, F.G., Maturana, H.R., Uribe, R.: Autopoiesis: the organization of living systems, its characterization and a model. Currents in modern biology 5(4), 187–196 (1974)
23. Buckl, S., Schweda, C.: A viable system perspective on enterprise architecture management. In: 2009 IEEE International Conference on Systems, Man, and Cybernetics (in publication, 2009)
24. Baas, N.A., Emmeche, C.: On emergence and explanation. Working Papers 97-02-008, Santa Fe Institute (1997)
25. de Boer, F.S., Bonsangue, M.M., Jacob, J., Stam, A., van der Torre, L.: Enterprise architecture analysis with xml. In: Proceedings of the 38th Annual Hawaii International Conference on System Sciences (HICSS 2005), vol. 8, p. 222b. IEEE Computer Society Press, Los Alamitos (2005)
26. Iacob, M.E., Jonkers, H.: Quantitative analysis of enterprise architectures. In: Konstantas, D., Bourrières, J.P., Léonard, M., Boudjlida, N. (eds.) Interoperability of Enterprise Software and Applications, Geneva, Switzerland, pp. 239–252. Springer, Heidelberg (2006)
27. Frank, U., Heise, D., Kattenstroth, H., Schauer, H.: Designing and utilising business indicator systems within enterprise models – outline of a method. In: Modellierung betrieblicher Informationssysteme (MobIS 2008) – Modellierung zwischen SOA und Compliance Management, Saarbrücken, Germany, November 27-28 (2008)

28. Johnson, P., Nordström, L., Lagerström, R.: Formalizing analysis of enterprise architecture. In: Interoperability for Enterprise Software and Applications Conference, Bordeaux, France, pp. 35–44. Springer, Heidelberg (2006)
29. Bucher, T., Fischer, R., Kurpjuweit, S., Winter, R.: Analysis and application scenarios of enterprise architecture: An exploratory study. In: Tenth IEEE International Enterprise Distributed Object Computing Conference (EDOC 2006), Hong Kong, China, Workshops, Washington, DC, USA, October 16-20. IEEE Computer Society, Los Alamitos (2006)
30. Kurpjuweit, S., Aier, S.: Ein allgemeiner Ansatz zur Ableitung von Abhängigkeitsanalysen auf Unternehmensarchitekturmodellen. In: 9. Internationale Tagung Wirtschaftsinformatik (WI 2007), Wien, Österreichische Computer Gesellschaft, pp. 129–138 (2009)
31. Yu, E., Strohmaier, M., Deng, X.: Exploring intentional modeling and analysis for enterprise architecture. In: Proceedings of the EDOC 2006 Conference Workshop on Trends in Enterprise Architecture Research (TEAR 2006), Hong Kong, p. 32. IEEE Computer Society Press, Los Alamitos (2006)
32. Yu, E.: Modelling strategic relationships for process reengineering. PhD thesis, University of Toronto, Toronto, Ont., Canada (1996)
33. Yu, E.: Towards modeling and reasoning support for early-phase requirements engineering. In: RE 1997: Proceedings of the 3rd IEEE International Symposium on Requirements Engineering, Washington, DC, USA. IEEE Computer Society, Los Alamitos (1997)
34. van Steenbergen, M., van den Berg, M., Brinkkemper, S.: An instrument for the development of the enterprise architecture practice. In: Cardoso, J., Cordeiro, J., Filipe, J. (eds.) ICEIS 2007 - Proceedings of the Ninth International Conference on Enterprise Information Systems, Volume EIS, Funchal, Madeira, Portugal, June 12-16, vol. 3, pp. 14–22 (2007)

# Guiding the Service Engineering Process: The Importance of Service Aspects

Qing Gu[1], Patricia Lago[1], and Elisabetta Di Nitto[2]

[1] Dept. of Computer Science, VU University Amsterdam, The Netherlands
{qinggu,patricia}@cs.vu.nl
[2] Dip. di Elettronica e Informazione, Politecnico di Milano, Italy
dinitto@elet.polimi.it

**Abstract.** Service-oriented System engineering (SOSE) and traditional software engineering mainly differ for their focus and aims. These differences are reflected by a number of aspects peculiar to SOSE (*service aspects*). In this paper we specifically discuss three service aspects: *the relevance of cross-organizational collaboration, increased importance of the identification of stakeholders*, and *the need for increased effort at run-/change time*. We argue that SOSE methodologies provide better guidance on their application when service aspects are emphasized in associated process models. By highlighting the three service aspects in a process model of the methodology defined in a large European project, we show specifically how each aspect provides guidance for engineering service-oriented systems in practice.

**Keywords:** Service-oriented system engineering, SOSE methodology, Process model, Service aspects.

## 1 Introduction

Service-oriented systems are constructed by integrating heterogeneous services that are developed using various programming languages and running on heterogeneous operating systems from a range of service providers [1]. The engineering of such systems is different from Traditional Software Engineering (TSE) in that: the *focus* is shifted from engineering applications to developing compositions of services; the *control of services* is passed from their users to other owners (i.e. users of services do not have the control of them), and the *aims* are not only to satisfy required functionality and quality (e.g. performance, security, maintainability) but also to have the ability of adapting to ever-changing requirements (e.g. flexibility, dynamicity).

Many SOSE methodologies have been proposed in both academia and industry aiming at providing approaches, methods and (sometimes) tools for researchers and practitioners to engineer service-oriented systems (see for instance [2]). However, without being fully understood, a methodology is less valuable no matter how perfect it is. This is particularly relevant to SOSE methodologies as they are more complex than TSE ones, having to deal with new challenges while keeping the principles of TSE. The additional complexity results mainly from open

R. Poler, M. van Sinderen, and R. Sanchis (Eds.): IWEI 2009, LNBIP 38, pp. 80–93, 2009.

world assumptions, co-existence of many stakeholders with conflicting requirements and the demand of adaptable systems [3].

To improve the understandability of a methodology and its guidance, software
development process models (describing what activities a development process
consists of and how they should be performed) have been often used since they
visualize the development process proposed by the methodology. The role of
process models is clearly identified in a survey [4] of leading model-based system
engineering methodologies, conducted by the INCOSE[1] community.

The service engineering community has realized that traditional software
process modeling techniques are no longer directly applicable or adaptable in
SOSE [5]. To overcome the mismatch between traditional software process models and SOSE, a number of service life cycle models have been proposed by both
industry and academia (e.g. [6,5,2,7]). However, none of the proposed models
has either reached a sufficient level of maturity or been able to fully express the
aspects that are peculiar to SOSE. Besides different names on the phases and
on the stakeholders, one might wonder what the real difference between these
models and many well defined and experimented TSE approaches is.

*Service aspects* are issues that are specifically relevant to SOSE. These aspects reveal the core distinctions between the service-oriented paradigm and the
traditional ones (e.g., component-based paradigm). Accordingly, the implication
of service aspects should be explicitly expressed in SOSE process models. For
instance, due to the dynamic nature of service-oriented systems, service artifacts (e.g. service specifications, service level agreements) are often generated
on the fly and used dynamically, whereas artifacts in TSE (e.g. requirements
specifications) are produced in a more static way, often within one single organization. Furthermore, service artifacts like service specifications are no longer
limited to local use; rather, they can be published, discovered and reused across
various SOSE projects [8] and activities scattered across multiple enterprises.
As a result, SOSE pays particular attention to the way loosely related activities
contribute to cross-organizational collaboration. Therefore, we argue that cross-
organizational collaboration should be specifically expressed in SOSE process
models to improve the guidance of applying SOSE methodologies.

In our previous work [7] we identified three service aspects that are crucial to
the SOSE development process, namely a) the relevance of cross-organizational
collaboration, b) the importance of the identification of stakeholders, and c) the
need for more effort at run- and change time. We also defined a stakeholder-
driven approach that illustrates such service aspects in a SOSE process model
developed from the literature.

Here we further build upon the previous work. In particular, we refine and
detail the service aspects and stress the necessity of expressing them in a SOSE
process model. With the aim of validating the service aspects and their relevance to SOSE, we modeled the methodology developed and used in the SeCSE[2]
European project. This has allowed us to: 1) build on concrete examples that

---

[1] www.incose.org/

[2] www.secse-project.eu

emphasize the relevance of the service aspects, and 2) show the applicability of the approach in practice. The results of this case study show that, by emphasizing service aspects in a SOSE process model, attention is naturally brought to those parts of the process model that are different as compared to TSE. The benefit is that guidance for applying a certain SOSE methodology is improved, and better service engineering management strategies can be put in place.

This work does not intend to propose a set of particular graphical notations for the purpose of modeling the SOSE development process. Instead, we intend to highlight *what* should be expressed in a SOSE process model. The graphical patterns (and associated notations) used in this paper illustrate one possible way of describing the service aspects expressively in a concrete SOSE process model.

The reminder of the paper is organized as follows. In Section 2, we explain the relevance of the service aspects to SOSE. In Section 3, we present the case study that we carried out and highlight the relevance of the three service aspects to the SeCSE methodology. Related work on the topic of SOSE process models is discussed in Section 4. Finally, Section 5 concludes the paper.

## 2   The Service Aspects

The fundamental change in developing service-oriented systems as opposed to traditional software systems is that software is delivered as a service. As such, users pay for and use services instead of buying and owning software. Consequently, users do not have the control of services, which are owned and controlled by service providers instead. These changes are reflected by three service aspects identified in [7]. In this section, we refine and detail these service aspects and stress the necessity of expressing them in a SOSE process model.

### 2.1   The Relevance of Cross-Organizational Collaboration

The focus of SOSE is shifted from applications to services that are collaboratively developed by multiple SOA roles [9,10], such as service consumer, service provider, service broker. During the development process, activities like specification&modeling, design, implementation, testing, operation and maintenance are all required to be performed in a collaborative manner [11].

For instance, service-oriented systems are built through discovering and composing existing services from multiple service providers rather than coding as in TSE. Consequently, the processes of discovering, selecting, composing services require continuous interaction (or *collaboration*) between the participating roles through the service development life cycle. Hence, collaboration between participating roles becomes *explicit* and *critical* in that it enters the details of a SOSE process that is now scattered across multiple roles. This makes their relationship tighter but also demanding clearer governance and agreements.

What makes it more critical is that these roles are often distributed in multiple departments or organizations. In this case, interactions between development activities associated with multiple business roles demand for collaboration between multiple organizations. We call this type of collaboration, which crosses the boundaries of the domain of each role, *cross-organizational collaboration*.

In TSE, and especially in concurrent software development, component-based software development, or outsourcing, cross-organizational collaboration also occurs when one organization delegates a set of tasks to the other organization(s). The main difference is that in TSE the first organization only concerns how software is developed internally, but not how delegated tasks are carried out externally. Consequently, only the results of the delegated tasks are of importance to the development process of the first organization. As a result, the cross-organizational collaboration is a purely *buying (outsourcer) and selling (supplier)* relationship, and its details are hidden from the perspective of the development process of the first organization. In SOSE, instead, the collaborative roles coexist in a service-oriented system rather than having an active-passive relationship. Detailed examples of the way in which coexisting roles collaborate are further discussed in Section 3.2.

When collaboration crosses the boundaries of each organization, barriers (e.g., conceptual, technological barriers, and organizational barriers) to enterprise interoperability often obstruct the effectiveness of collaboration. Since collaboration between multiple roles becomes part of the SOSE process, it is of great importance to highlight this collaboration in a SOSE process model. When the collaboration becomes explicit and clear, the need for corresponding agreements or contracts becomes evident. Consequently, appropriate governance can be applied. As such, barriers to enterprise interoperability can be reduced.

## 2.2  Increased Importance of the Identification of Stakeholders

A *stakeholder* can be defined as a person, group or organization playing a well defined role (or roles) in a SOSE methodology. Since cross-organizational collaboration becomes more critical in SOSE, the importance of clearly identifying stakeholders increases accordingly. If stakeholders are identified at a too coarse granularity, the represented interaction remains not fully specified. This leads to unclear responsibilities among collaborating enterprises and thus decrease in trust and possibly in success. Because the level of details matters, the identification of stakeholders directly determines the level of detail expressed in a SOSE process model.

The decision on whether a role should be identified as a separate stakeholder in a SOSE process model depends on what type of interactions the model intends to represent. For instance, if a SOSE development approach intends to emphasize or elaborate on how service monitoring is provided, accordingly, service monitor could be selected as a stakeholder in a SOSE process model. As such, it offers the possibility to explicitly associate monitoring-related activities with the service monitor and to explicitly describe the interaction between the service monitor and other stakeholders. Of course, if service monitoring is not the main focus, then it is not necessary to select it as a separate stakeholder since the detailed interaction between a service monitor and the other stakeholders is not of interest.

As a general rule, if service monitoring (or any other activity) is performed by an independent third party, the corresponding role should better be identified as a separate stakeholder because it stands for an external organization. As such, it offers the possibility to explicitly express the responsibilities across different business domains.

The importance of the identification of stakeholders in SOSE process models also lies in the fact that stakeholders in the SOSE development process do not always assume the same roles as in TSE. For instance, in general a software developer is responsible for coding or implementing software applications, while in SOSE a service developer could be responsible also for composing existing services, depending on specific methodologies. Without specifically associating SOSE activities to stakeholders, one is not able to visualize the corresponding responsibilities as one would do in TSE.

In summary, identifying stakeholders with the appropriate level of detail in a SOSE development approach facilitates the establishment of a corresponding SOSE process model describing associated activities and their interactions at an appropriate level of abstraction.

### 2.3   The Need for Increased Effort at Run-/Change Time

In TSE, the main goal is to develop high quality applications that meet the requirements of the end users. Consequently, most of the effort is dedicated to design (collecting requirements, design, and implementation) and change time (maintenance). Runtime activities are hardly addressed if not in specific domains. Furthermore, change time activities are often performed off line (either with or without execution interruption).

Different than TSE, the main goal of SOSE is not only to deliver high quality but also agile and robust services which are able to meet the *ever-changing* business requirements. Consequently, much more development effort is shifting from design time to run-/change time. For instance, components identification is often performed at design time in TSE; the SOSE equivalent activity is service discovery, which is encouraged to be performed at runtime and it is regarded as one of the major challenges in the SOSE field.

As discussed in Section 4, most existing SOSE process models do fail in emphasizing this shift. By explicitly modeling the two stages, a process model can visualize the amount of activities shifted to run-/change time, hence providing useful inputs to resource allocation.

## 3   Applying Service Aspects to a Concrete Methodology

With the aim of gaining insight in the extent to which the modeling of the three service aspects improve the guidance of a SOSE development approach, we modeled them in a concrete and practical context, i.e. the SeCSE methodology [12].

In this section, we first introduce the SeCSE methodology and present its process model (with the three service aspects being highlighted), followed by a discussion of how each service aspect both emphasizes the characteristics of the SeCSE methodology itself and facilitates better SOSE guidance.

## 3.1   The SeCSE Methodology

The SeCSE project is a EU-funded project. Its goal was to investigate methods, techniques and tools to develop and manage service-oriented systems in an effective way. A large number of academic and industrial partners have been collaborating in this project. As a consequence, the resulting SeCSE methodology has both theoretical and practical value.

The SeCSE methodology describes the main development activities and tools that have been adopted by the SeCSE project. It provides ways to create service compositions where component services are discovered at runtime either on the basis of the context of usage or when a certain service fails. This focus on runtime is one step forward towards the third generation service-oriented systems [13].

Although service discovery is regarded as one of the major activities in developing service-oriented systems, and even though techniques already exist to support service discovery, in practice service discovery is hardly adopted. Nowadays, most enterprises focus on migrating legacy systems to service-oriented systems and implementing new services rather than discovering services from a registry (as service-oriented systems are supposed to do). In the SeCSE project, service discovery is not only addressed by the SeCSE methodology, but also experimented in the consortium. As an advanced and relatively mature approach, the SeCSE methodology is a good candidate to be selected as the case study in this work to analyze the service aspects addressed by it.

Moreover, the design of the SeCSE methodology does not specifically or consciously take our three service aspects into consideration. This provides us the possibility to take the SeCSE methodology as such and model the service aspects addressed by the methodology. Comparing to the original process model illustrated in the documentation of the SeCSE methodology, the SeCSE process model proposed in this work provides better guidance for its users.

## 3.2   The SOSE Process Model for the SeCSE Methodology

By focusing on service aspects, our main objective is to discuss *what* has to be modeled rather than *how* to model. For illustration purposes, we use BPMN[3] as process modeling notation to be used to communicate a methodology to its users. This is expressive enough to represent the various inter-dependencies and multiple stakeholders involved in the SeCSE development process.

For the purpose of modeling the service aspects of the SeCSE methodology, we illustrated the SeCSE development process by means of a process model. The decisions and assumptions that we have made to construct the SeCSE process

---

[3] www.omg.org/spec/BPMN/

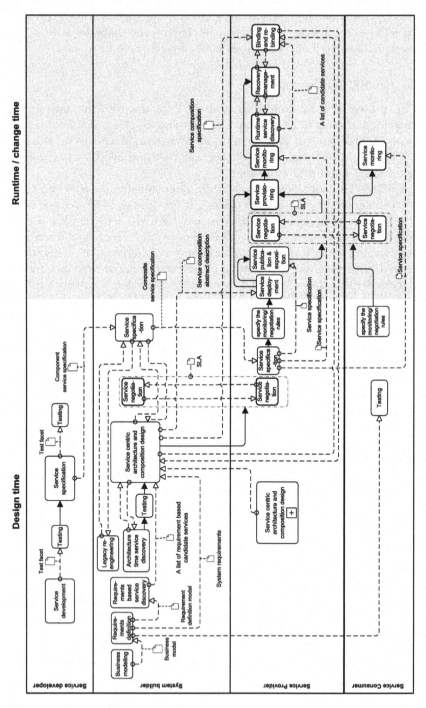

**Fig. 1.** The SOSE process model for the SeCSE methodology

model were verified with the SeCSE experts to check for correspondence of the model to the methodology. This analysis has also helped to elicit information that were missing or left implicit in the methodology document. After the verification from the SeCSE experts, we were able to refine and finalize the model[4].

The resulting model is given in Fig. 1. In this model, we specifically modeled the stakeholders identified in the SeCSE methodology to highlight the *increased importance of the identification of stakeholders*; we specifically modeled their associated activities and inter-dependencies to highlight the *cross-organizational collaboration*. The *increased effort at run-/change time* becomes obvious in the model since we separated them from the design time effort.

For each service aspect we first explain its associated graphical pattern in a SOSE process model in general; and then we discuss how the SeCSE methodology addresses the service aspect by observing the SeCSE process model against the graphical pattern.

**The Relevance of Cross-Organizational Collaboration.** Fig. 2 graphically illustrates the cross-organizational collaboration (COC) service aspect. The left-hand side of the figure shows three collaboration types (COC patterns): *peer activities group, main-sub activities* and *distributed activities*. These patterns are exemplified in the right-hand side of Fig. 2.

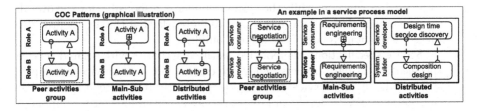

**Fig. 2.** Service aspect: cross-organizational collaboration (COC)

- The **peer activities group** models same activities carried out *in parallel* across multiple partner enterprises. For instance, service negotiation can be carried out by a service provider and a service consumer with the common objective of reaching the agreement of service provision and consumption.
- The **main-sub activities** model the same activities carried out *partially by one partner enterprise and completed by another*. For instance, a service consumer may perform the user-centric part of a requirement engineering activity that the service provider is mainly responsible for.
- The **distributed activities** model *inter-dependent activities carried out across multiple partner enterprises*. For instance, design time service discovery can be carried out by a service developer and composition design can be carried out by a system builder. The former provides input (such as discovered candidate services) to the latter; the latter might also provide feedback

---

[4] Due to the limited space, the design of the case study itself is not described in detail.

to the former when different design decisions are taken, possibly requiring different service candidates.

By observing the SeCSE process model (shown in Fig. 1) against the three COC patterns defined in Fig. 2, the attention is brought to specific types of cross-organizational collaboration.

- **Peer activities group:** Service negotiation occurs twice in the SeCSE development process. One is carried out by a service provider and a service consumer; another is carried out by a system builder and a service provider. By nature, each service negotiation must be performed in parallel by both its stakeholders as peers. The results of the collaborations (indicated by the data objects attached to the peers) are SLAs. Different from TSE where contracts are often established after software is built, SLAs in SOSE often precede final service products (service composition in the case of the SeCSE methodology). These SLAs are also potentially useful to other activities such as service monitoring.
- **Main-sub activities:** Service centric architecture and composition design are carried out by a system builder and service provider in a cooperative manner. A system builder has the main responsibility for this activity, whereas a service provider focuses only on a subset of its tasks. For instance, the service provider might work on the definition of the list of possible candidate services to be used at runtime; while the system builder is responsible for the overall service composition design. In this way, the subtasks that the service provider takes are of competence of the system builder.

  Service specifications are modeled as three activities with related service specification as data objects. They are carried out by a service developer, system builder and service provider independently but on related artifacts. In general, a service developer creates service specifications for a component service, which influences a composite service carried out by a system builder. The system builder has to make sure that the QoS characteristics defined in the specification of the component services are compatible with those of the composite service. When a service composition or a single service is deployed, the service provider may add information to the corresponding specification known at deployment time.
- **Distributed activities:** Service centric architecture and composition design is carried out by a system builder at design time and binding and re-binding is carried out by a service provider at run-/change time. Cross-organizational collaboration occurs when new substituting services are discovered at run time (e.g., due to a new requirement) and service composition needs to update its bindings to accommodate the change.

Only when the collaboration is explicitly captured, the stakeholders of service-oriented systems can gain insight on the impact between their own responsibilities and the others'. Each stakeholder has a clearer view on at what time ( *"when"*) which activity ( *"what"*) has to be carried out in cooperation with which stakeholder ( *"who"*) and in which manner ( *"how"*). In the SOSE development process, external enterprises often continuously play important roles throughout the service life cycle. By looking for the cross-organizational collaboration patterns in a service process model, enterprises are brought to focus on the points needing strategic business agreements that should regulate such tight collaboration.

**Increased Importance of the Identification of Stakeholders.** Fig. 3 graphically represents the stakeholders pattern (and an example), which makes the stakeholders in a SOSE process model explicit. By observing the SeCSE process model (shown in Fig. 1) against this stakeholder pattern, we can see that the SeCSE methodology involves mainly four stakeholders, namely: service developer, system builder, service provider and service consumer). These stakeholders, potentially representing partner enterprises, play common SOA roles from the perspective of service implementation, integration provision, and consumption.

Explicitly modeling the identified stakeholders improves the guidance of the SeCSE methodology as follows. Firstly, by placing the SOSE activities in the corresponding swimlanes, the SeCSE process model naturally shows the responsibilities and collaborations of and among stakeholders. This is especially crucial in SOSE where cross-organizational collaboration occurs in almost all activities. In this way, the business dependencies requiring contractual/SLA agreements are made explicit, and project managers can better plan the allocation of development activities based on the skills and responsibilities of the internal and external stakeholders.

Secondly, service composition centered characteristic of the SeCSE methodology is well captured by the SeCSE process model when identified stakeholders are explicitly modeled. Fig. 1 shows that most of the development activities are associated to the system builder and the service provider (stakeholders that carry out service composition activities). Furthermore, the model shows that the system builder and the service provider are tightly linked; the service developer and the service consumer are instead loosely linked. Due to focus of service composition, the service consumer in the SeCSE process model is considered as the consumer of composite services, rather than the consumer of component services. Therefore, the service consumer does not have direct interaction with the service developer, and the system builder must cooperate with the service provider in multiple activities. In this way, the SeCSE process model very well captures the fact that service composition is the main focus of the SeCSE methodology and consequently provides better guidance in that the stakeholders are able to gain better understanding of the focus of the (SeCSE) methodology.

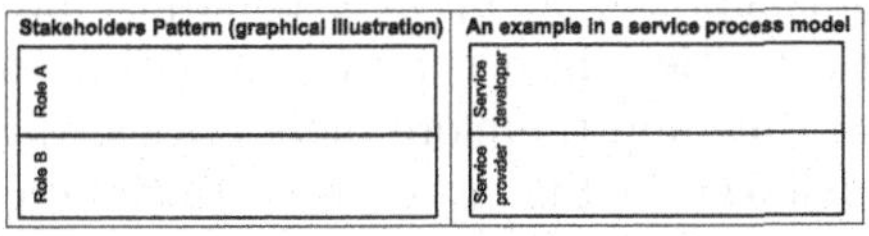

**Fig. 3.** Service aspect: increased importance of the identification of stakeholders

**The Need for Increased Effort at Run-/Change Time.** Our approach of separating the design and run-/change time activities in a SOSE process model is presented in Fig 4, where the left-hand side of the figure shows the 2-stages pattern, exemplified in the right-hand side of the figure. In this example, it is visually evident that service design is carried out at design time; while service discovery is performed at run-/change time.

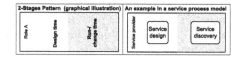

**Fig. 4.** Service aspect: increased effort at run-/change time (2-Stages)

By observing the SeCSE process model (shown in Fig. 1) against the 2-stages pattern defined in Fig. 4, we are now able to easily distinguish the design time activities (falling in the left-hand side of the figure) from the run-/change time activities (in the shadowed area at the right-hand side of the figure). Consequently, the guidance for applying the SeCSE methodology is improved in that the process model shows its support for adaptation, service composition and facilitates critical project plan decisions.

Firstly, we notice that about one third of the development effort is dedicated to run-/change time activities. In particular, runtime service discovery and service negotiation are supported by the SeCSE methodology with the objective of increasing the adaptability and agility of resulting systems to meet on-the-fly requirements. Thereby, related activities such as runtime service monitoring, recovery management, and binding and re-binding are also in place.

Secondly, we notice that the development effort dedicated to run-/change time activities is not evenly distributed among the stakeholders in the SeCSE methodology. Instead, the service provider carries out most of the run-/change time activities; while the system builder and service developer do not perform run-/change time activities at all. We have discussed in Section 3.2 that the roles of system builder and service provider are extensively developed due to the service composition centered approach. The process model illustrates and emphasizes further the separation of design and run-/change time activities: the system builder focuses on the design of service compositions; while the service provider focuses on the provision of service compositions.

Thirdly, knowing which activities are executed at which stage is also crucial in SOSE. Project managers should be able to adjust project plans based on the criticality of the activities since runtime activities are directly related to executing services real-time and therefore more critical than design time activities. For instance, as shown in Fig. 1 service negotiation is supported by the SeCSE methodology at both design time and runtime. The difference is that at design time, service negotiation occurs between a system builder and a service provider for component services that are selected for service composition;

at runtime it occurs between a service provider and a service consumer for a composite service that fulfills business requirements. This difference results in different levels of business commitment. At design time, the failure of reaching service level agreements or the failure of collaborating with a service provider does not have huge business impact on the system builder; the system builder can always decide to look for an alternative service. However, at runtime if the composite service fails to execute or does not reach the quality it promises, the system builder faces risks to loose its customer and even its business market. Here, the business commitment is much higher than at design time. Being aware of this difference, a project manager is able to decide which actions to take for activities with various levels of criticality.

**Summary.** As auspicated, highlighting the service aspects in the SeCSE process model allows those who have to exploit the methodology to have more clear evidence of issues (cooperation between organizations, numerous stakeholders, activities to be executed during the operaton phase) that are critical from the managerial point of view. By observing the service aspects captured in the model, we may conclude (and becomes more evident) that some differences between SOSE and TSE become obvious in the applied SeCSE context. Firstly, the fact that each of the four identified stakeholders is responsible for a common SOA role (centered on services) reflects the shifted focus from applications to service pools. Secondly, due to the fact that consumers of services do not have the control of them, more interactions between stakeholders (cross-organizational collaboration) occur, as shown by the many arrows crossing the various swimlanes. Thirdly, around one third of activities are carried out at run-/change time, which shows that resulting systems are dynamic and therefore have the potential ability to adapt to ever-changing requirements.

## 4   Related Work

It has been gradually recognized that traditional software process models are no longer sufficient to model the SOSE development process. To overcome the mismatch between traditional process models and the SOSE development process, a number of SOSE-specific process models have been proposed by both industry and academia. However, as we already discussed in [7], these assume that the development of service-oriented systems is entirely internal to an organization. For instance, the model proposed by IBM in [6] describes four phases that are implicitly assumed to be executed by IBM itself or any organization adopting the IBM methodology. This results in the fact that the actual difference between SOSE and TSE methodologies remain unclear. As discussed in Section 2, we argue instead that interactions across the organizational boundaries require in SOSE particular attention, and should be made explicit.

While the approaches found in the literature are proposals of specific methodologies and lifecycles, our approach can be seen as a way to interpret and investigate different existing lifecycles. This has a value per se as it does not force people to adopt a specific approach for developing and managing service-oriented systems, but it helps them to understand and make coherent all the methods they use in their common practice. In a similar line of research, Blake in [5] advocates the distinction between two key activities: service development and service-centric system management. While the first activity follows a quite traditional iterative process, service-centric system management is seen as much more dynamic of the traditional processes associated with the development and the operation of other kinds of software. In particular, as in SeCSE, runtime (sub)activities such as re-binding are identified. The importance of stakeholders is stressed, and a number of them is identified and assigned to the various activities of the lifecycle. We differentiate from this work as we highlight not only stakeholders and their activities, but also the interaction between these stakeholders and the artifacts they produce and exchange. As we have argued in the previous sections, in fact, clarifying these aspects help all roles involved in the lifecycle in better understanding the critical aspects of the lifecycle and in properly drive it toward the achievement of the project goal.

Bell [14] proposes the structure of a SOSE process model, which consists of timeline, events, seasons and disciplines. As we do, he uses timelines to indicate a sequence of development activities. Design and run-/change time activities in our approach correspond to seasons in Bells structure, while our development activities can be regarded as disciplines in Bells structure. The approach is also focusing on defining and classifying those events that have an impact on the lifecycle. While a differentiation between runtime and design time activities is presented, all runtime aspects are not described in detail. Also, the approach does not seem to stress the aspects related to the interaction between the stakeholders that we consider of paramount importance.

## 5   Conclusions

In this paper, we emphasize the importance of explicitly expressing in process models service aspects that are peculiar to SOSE. We argue that having these service aspects highlighted would provide better guidance on the SOSE development process. We have applied our service aspects on a concrete SOSE methodology. The results show that these service aspects help understanding the SOSE methodology when they are made explicit in an associated process model. Moreover, the use of the methodology and project management are also facilitated.

Further, these service aspects emphasize the SOSE support of a certain methodology. In this way, they help identifying if the methodology itself will deliver 'real' service-oriented systems. For instance, by analyzing these service aspects in the SeCSE methodology, we can see that: it involves the standard SOA roles; it covers the interaction among these roles; and it pays particular attention to run-/change time activities. We therefore argue that the service-oriented systems it delivers would potentially be dynamic, agile and have good alignment to business requirements.

# Acknowledgments

The research leading to these results has received funding from the European Community's Seventh Framework Programme FP7/2007-2013 under grant agreement 215483 (S-Cube).

# References

1. Papazoglou, M.P.: Service-oriented computing: Concepts, characteristics and directions. In: Proceedings of the Fourth International Conference on Web Information Systems Engineering (WISE). IEEE Computer Society, Los Alamitos (2003)
2. Papazoglou, M.P., van den Heuvel, W.J.: Service-oriented design and development methodology. Int. J. Web Engineering and Technology (IJWET) 2(4), 412–442 (2006)
3. Baresi, L., Nitto, E.D., Ghezzi, C.: Toward open-world software: Issues and challenges. IEEE Computer Society 39(10), 36–43 (2006)
4. Estefan, J.A.: Survey of model-based systems engineering (MBSE) methodologies, Jet Propulsion Laboratory, California Institute of Technology, Pasedena, CA (2007)
5. Blake, M.B.: Decomposing composition: Service-Oriented software engineers. IEEE Software 24(6), 68–77 (2007)
6. McBride, G.: The role of SOA quality management in SOA service lifecycle management. developerWorks (2007)
7. Gu, Q., Lago, P.: A stakeholder-driven service life cycle model for SOA. In: IW-SOSWE 2007: 2nd international workshop on Service oriented software engineering, Dubrovnik, Croatia, pp. 1–7. ACM, New York (2007)
8. Tsai, W.T., Jin, Z., Wang, P., Wu, B.: Requirement engineering in service-oriented system engineering. In: ICEBE 2007. Proceedings of the IEEE International Conference on e-Business Engineering. IEEE Computer Society, Los Alamitos (2007)
9. Tsai, W.T., Wei, X., Paul, R., Chung, J.Y., Huang, Q., Chen, Y.: Service-oriented system engineering (SOSE) and its applications to embedded system development. Service Oriented Computing and Applications, 3–17 (2007)
10. Colombo, M.M., Nitto, E.D., Penta, M.D., Distante, D., Zuccala, M.: Speaking a common language: A conceptual model for describing service-oriented systems. In: Benatallah, B., Casati, F., Traverso, P. (eds.) ICSOC 2005. LNCS, vol. 3826, pp. 48–60. Springer, Heidelberg (2005)
11. Tsai, W.T.: Service-oriented system engineering: A new paradigm. In: Service-Oriented System Engineering, Beijing, China, pp. 3–6 (2005)
12. Penta, M.D., Bastida, L., Sillitti, A., Baresi, L., Ripa, G., Melideo, M., Tilly, M., Spanoudakis, G., Maiden, N., Cruz, J.G., Hutchinson, J.: SeCSE - Service Centric System Engineering: an overview. At your service: Service Engineering in the Information Society Technologies Program (2009)
13. Fitzgerald, B., Olsson, C.M.: The software and services challenge. In: EY 7th Framework Programme, Contribution to the preparation of the Technology Pillar on "Software, Grids, Security and Dependability" (2006)
14. Bell, M.: Service-Oriented Modeling (SOA): Service Analysis, Design, and Architecture. Wiley, Chichester (2008)

# From Business Value Model to Coordination Process Model

Hassan Fatemi, Marten van Sinderen, and Roel Wieringa

Information Systems (IS) Research Group,
Electrical Engineering, Mathematics and Computer Science (EEMCS) Department,
University of Twente, Enschede, The Netherlands
h.fatemi@utwente.nl, m.j.vansinderen@ewi.utwente.nl, roelw@cs.utwente.nl

**Abstract.** The increased complexity of business webs calls for modeling the collaboration of enterprises from different perspectives, in particular the business and process perspectives, and for mutually aligning these perspectives. Business value modeling and coordination process modeling both are necessary for a good e-business design, but these activities have different goals and use different concepts. Nevertheless, the resulting models should be consistent with each other because they refer to the same system from different perspectives. Hence, checking the consistency between these models or producing one based on the other would be of high value. In this paper we discuss the issue of achieving consistency in multi-level e-business design and give guidelines to produce consistent coordination process models from business value models in a stepwise manner.

**Keywords:** Business value modeling, coordination process modeling, consistency checking, enterprise interoperability.

## 1 Introduction

Today, enterprises operate more and more together in networked collaborations rather than just on their own. There are many reasons for this. Among others we can refer to more complicated user needs, upward tendency toward specialization, changing customer demands, higher customer satisfaction indexes, etc. In the literature collections of enterprises that jointly satisfy a complex consumer need, are called business webs [1]. In a business web each enterprise contributes with its own specific expertise, products and services to satisfy a consumer need. For example, a web shop, logistics company, payment provider and authentication provider can jointly provide the service of on-line buying to consumers. Each partner wants to be sure that participation in such a collaboration network is economically profitable and sustainable before operational details of the coordination infrastructure are being designed. This is where business modeling comes into play. A coordination process model will be designed only if the business case is positive for each of the partners.

A coordination process model should specify the coordination activities (in terms of message exchanges) necessary to make the collaboration work. But,

R. Poler, M. van Sinderen, and R. Sanchis (Eds.): IWEI 2009, LNBIP 38, pp. 94–106, 2009.

it is hard to design a coordination process model based on a business value model only, because there is a large conceptual gap between these two models [2]. The main goal of business value modeling is to reach agreement amongst stakeholders regarding the question "Who is offering what of value to whom and expects what of value in return?" In contrast, an important goal of coordination process modeling is to reach a common understanding about which coordination activities should be carried out, and in which order. Business value modeling focuses on modeling economic sustainability of e-business while coordination process modeling focuses on modeling operational fulfillment. These are two different modeling goals, asking for different modeling methods with different constructs.

The research question addressed in this paper is: how to achieve consistency between business value models and coordination process models. The contribution of this paper consists of the description of initial guidelines to produce a coordination process model from a given business value model.

For representing the business value perspective, we use value models of $e^3value$ [3], and for the coordination process perspective, we use BPMN diagrams (see http://www.bpmn.org/). Our choice for $e^3value$ is motivated by the fact that it can express value transfers and value objects in general, as well as business actors. Our guidelines can be applied to any notation that can express this, but currently there is no other language that can express these things. The choice for BPMN is motivated by the fact that it is easy to read and well-known. Our guidelines can however be used with any other coordination language.

In section 2, we discuss the previous work published on this issue. Then, in section 3, we discuss about business value modeling and coordination process modeling and enumerate their similarities and differences. Based on these findings, we propose a stepwise approach to generate a coordination process model from a business value model in section 4. In section 5, we will apply our method on a case study and then analyze the results in section 6. Finally we conclude with a discussion of results and future research in section 7.

## 2   Related Work

The current approaches that consider the conceptual gap between business value models and coordination process models can be classified in two main groups:

- **Consistency Checkers:** These approaches assume that we have two models (a business value model and a coordination process model) of the same system and all we want is checking whether they are consistent with each other or not? Most of these approaches have solely considered consistency checking of static aspects, i.e., during design time and do not consider the runtime behavior of a model [4,5,6]. Bodenstaff [7,8] has introduced another approach toward consistency checking by considering the runtime behavior of the coordination process models. These approaches don't use the same definition for consistency and none of them is comprehensive enough to justify the consistency of these two models solely.

- **Model Generators:** These approaches don't assume the availability of both a business value model and a coordination process model of the same system. Hence, they try to produce one from the other (mostly a coordination process model from a business value model) so that in the end both models be consistent with each other [9,10,11].

  Pijpers and Gordijn proposed a method that makes an intermediate model ($e^3 transition$ model) based on the business value model by extending it with independent transfers of *ownership rights* of an object and the actual object itself.

  Anderson and Bergholtz proposed a method that starts with a business value model and in a number of steps, each value exchange is analyzed and identified as a sub-process of the coordination process model. They break value exchanges to components (resource, right, custody, and document evidence).

  Wieringa et al. claim that coordination modeling is facilitated by making a *physical delivery model* first, because the business and coordination model are both views of a network of physical deliveries. They distinguish *discrete* from *cumulative* goods and *time continuous* from *time-discrete* deliveries. They also specify frequency or duration of deliveries and make a *delivery model* as an intermediate model on the way to design a coordination process model.

In our opinion, these approaches are all too complicated because they ask for additional models and use complicated concepts such as ownership right, custody and physical delivery that makes it hard for others to use them in practice. Our proposed method is simpler, more general and comprehensive. By keeping it simple, we try to increase its applicability by other people.

## 3    Business Value Models and Coordination Process Models

As mentioned before, (business) value models and coordination (process) models are two models of the same system from different perspectives. A value model focuses on high level and static objects (e.g. value objects and actors) and value exchanges, while in contrast, a coordination model focuses on procedural details mainly message exchanges. A value model is built first because in that way participating companies can know as early as possible whether the cooperation will be economically sustainable for each of the partners. $e^3 value$ is to our knowledge the only method that can do this with the level of formality that we need in order to be able to talk about consistency with coordination modeling.

In this section, we will pave the ground for the proposed method by enumerating the similarities and differences between value modeling and coordination modeling. Consider the $e^3 value$ model (figure 1(a)) and its corespondent coordination model in BPMN notation (figure 1(c)), in which a *buyer* a *seller* and a *transporter* exchange some values. The *buyer* gives *money* to the *seller* and receives *good* in return. The *seller*, in turn, gives *money* to the *transporter* and receives *transport*. We will discuss these models in detail later.

### 3.1   Differences

The conceptual gap between value models and coordination models is caused mostly by the following properties of these models:

1. **Ordering:** The key concept in value modeling is *value* while its counterpart in coordination modelling is *time*. In an $e^3value$ model there is no notion of time ordering at all [3]. The goal of a value model is to understand economic reciprocity of value transfers and to analyze the economic sustainability and profitability of the value activities of the actors. Behavior and temporal order are beyond the value perspective and are part of the coordination perspective. In addition, in value models there is no specific notion of cardinality or duration of value transfers and also it does not express preconditions of value transfers. But specifying preconditions of value transfers are an important part of business contracts.

2. **Value versus coordination objects:** In a value model every object should be of value to at least one partner (value object). Hence, there will be no place in a value model for those objects that are not of value to a partner. But in a coordination model objects are not included necessarily because they are of economic value to a partner. They can also be included because they help coordinating the activities of the partners. For example, *messages* are common objects that are used frequently in coordination models but, they don't have a particular economic value for any partner. Hence, they have no counterpart in value models. We call objects in the coordination model *coordination objects*.

3. **Third parties:** A direct value exchange between two partners in a value model does not necessarily imply that there will be a direct control object exchange between these partners in the corresponding coordination model. Sometimes a third party will be involved and the path for value object exchange becomes an indirect path for control object exchange. A well-known example for this case is the relation between buyer, seller and transporter in value model and coordination model. In this setting, there is a direct value exchange between the buyer and the seller, while the physical transfer of the good that is the subject of the value exchange will require an indirect control object exchange between the buyer and the seller involving a transporter. All three actors are present in a value model as well as in a coordination model, but the economic value interactions differ from the coordination interactions (see figure 1).

4. **Paying methods:** Money transfers are the most common transfers in value models that indicate paying a partner some money in exchange of his/her service or good. A money transfer between two partners in the value model, does not imply the paying method. There is a wide variety of payment methods for services and goods and this must be represented in the coordination model.

When moving from one type of model to the other, conceptual gap caused by the above four factors may have to be bridged.

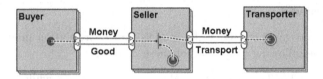

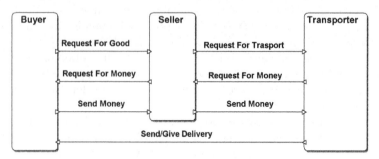

(a) Business Value model of Buyer, Seller and Transporter

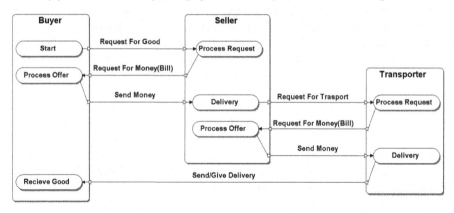

(b) All interactions (messages) Between Buyer, Seller and Transporter

(c) Coordination Process model of Buyer, Seller and Transporter

**Fig. 1.** From Business Value model to Coordination Process model

## 3.2   Similarities

Despite the aforementioned conceptual gap, value modeling and coordination modeling also address some common aspects. First of all, they have the same actors/partners. In the business world, a partner joins a group only if (s)he earns something of value to herself/himself. Hence, every actor in a business network perceives some value and therefore will be present in the value model independently or as a part of another actor/partner. Because we are only interested in the way that independent actors cooperate with each other, rather than the internal organizational process, the coordination model contains only ordered interactions between independent actors.

Secondly, each value exchange, consisting of value transfers between two partners in different directions, indicates that something should happen to realize them. Different ways can be imagined to realize a value exchange. To start, we make some simplifying assumptions to reduce the complexity of the problem and converge different solutions.

In the coordination model we don't mention the activities that are internal to an actor, i.e. activities that don't involve communication with another actor. We don't take into consideration every necessary measure in message exchanges. For example when actor $A$ contacts actor $B$ three interactions can be imagined. First $A$ sends a request to $B$, then $B$ sends back a confirmation that it has received the request, and finally $A$ sends back $B$ the final confirmation. These interactions are necessary especially from the legal point of view in particular in situations that involve money transfers. But here for the sake of simplicity we have abstracted from them. This does not decrease the utility of our guidelines because any set of interactions between two actors can be preceded by a set of setup interactions without creating an inconsistency with the value model.

An important simplifying assumption is that all actors are trusted so that we don't need to consider security mechanisms to avoid mitigate the risk of frauds. In a realistic business model this assumption needs to be dropped but before building such a realistic model, the partners need to check whether the cooperation is economically sustainable (value model) and practically possible (coordination model) under the assumption that they can trust each other. If economic sustainability and practical possibility cannot be shown under the assumption of mutual trust, it is not worth the effort to check this under the more complicated conditions of lack of trust [12]. In this paper we therefore make this simplifying assumption but in future work we will drop it.

## 4    From a Value Model to a Coordination Model

The analysis above (section 3) will give a basis for the proposed method. The starting point is an $e^3value$ model. As an example, we consider the $e^3value$ model in figure 1(a).

**Step 1:** The first step is identifying the actors of the coordination model. As said in section 3.2 the actors in both value model and coordination model must be the same (buyer, seller, and transporter).

**Step 2:** In this step we aim at determining the necessary interactions that should be included in the coordination model to realize value exchanges. Under the simplifying assumptions mentioned in section 3.2, for each value transfer a pair of interactions (coordination objects) are enough to realize it. This pair consists of a request message and a message referring to the actual value object of the corresponding value transfer. Hence, we need four interactions for realizing each value exchange in the value model. In this way we cover the gap caused by the conceptual difference between value objects in the value model and coordination objects in the coordination model.

There is a special type of value exchange, which we call *scheduled exchanges*, that is excluded from this rule. An example of this type of value exchange is scheduled payment in which a partner pays an already determined amount of money for a service/good on already scheduled times. In these cases no party asks the other one for paying the money. Hence, in these cases in the coordination model we have only two interactions referring to the actual value objects.

**Step 3:** In this step we consider the third factor of the gap between value models and coordination models , namely *third parties*. For this purpose, we consider the following questions:

1. *Who should send a request to whom? (Which partner to which other one?)*
2. *Who should give value to whom? (Which partner to which other one?)*

In most of the cases, when there are no third parties in realizing value exchange, the answers to these questions are obvious and straightforward. In these cases, the partner that is going to receive the value object, sends a request message to the other one, that is going to send it, and then the latter sends the actual value to the requester. However, when third parties are involved in the process, we should exactly determine the sender and the receiver of the request message and the value object (See figure 1(b)). This model is an interaction model that shows who is causing the transfer of some observable object to whom.

At this point we see all the necessary interactions between partners, but still without any time ordering, so it is not yet a coordination model. Our next goal is to put these interactions in some ordering relationship and also determine the duration or cardinality of each of them.

**Step 4:** In order to put the interactions in a correct order in the coordination model we have to ask the following two questions regarding each value exchange of the value model:

1. *Who should first send a request to whom? (Which partner initiates?)*
2. *Which value transfer should happen first?*

Using the answers to these two questions we can put the four interactions in a correct order. Suppose that, for the case at hand, we have the following answers to the above two questions respectively:

1. *The buyer should first send a request to the seller.*
2. *The seller gives the good to the buyer via the transporter.*

The first answer is obvious and it indicates a request message from the buyer to the seller in the coordination model. However, the second answer indicates that the seller will not send the good to the buyer by himself/herself. Instead, (s)he should ask the transporter to do it. In other words, the seller should send a request message to the transporter to transport the good.

**Step 5**: After identifying the necessary interactions and putting them in the coordination model in a correct order, we can ask questions about time constraints to determine duration or cardinality characteristics of interactions. Using the answers to these questions, we can design the exact coordination model for the value model at hand. For example, suppose that $A$ provides service $S$ to $B$ for 1 year, and $B$ pays $A$ some money every month. In this case after including the necessary interactions in a correct order to the coordination model, we should add the duration property of the provisioning of the service and cardinality property of the payment.

**Step 6**: In this step we finalize the coordination model by adding the necessary and appropriate activities to each partner in order to link together the included interactions. In this way, starting from the partner with the start_stimulus (small circle), in the value model,we go forward in the model till we reach the partners with the end_stimulus (bull's eye). Now, the *start* and the *stop* activities can also be added to the model (See figure 1(c)).

# 5   Case Study

To check whether our method indeed delivers a coordination model that is consistent its correspondent value model in a non-trivial case, we took an example that deals with the problem of clearing Intellectual Property Rights (IPR). It involves two steps: collecting fees from IPR users, i.e. radio stations, bars, discotheques and so on, and repartitioning the collected fees to Right Owners, i.e. artists, song writers, producers. The main IPR society interested in this problem is SENA (see http://www.sena.nl/).

Since 1993 SENA has been designated by the Ministry of Justice of The Netherlands to take care of the Neighboring Rights not only for Dutch right owners but also for foreign right owners of the music tracks in The Netherlands. It means whenever a track is played in public spaces with the aim of getting money from it, SENA must collect fees from such entities making money (IPR users) and repartition these fees to right owners (IPR owners). The aim is a pay-per-play scenario. It means that for each music track, a track-specific network of clearing organizations must be composed.

## 5.1   Value Model

The business model is based on the $e^3value$ methodology. The actors are:

**Receivers:** A receiver is an actor who broadcasts background music to get benefits of it so, they are also IPR users.

**Background Music Providers (BMP):** A BMP is an actor who provides specialized background music in exchange of fee.

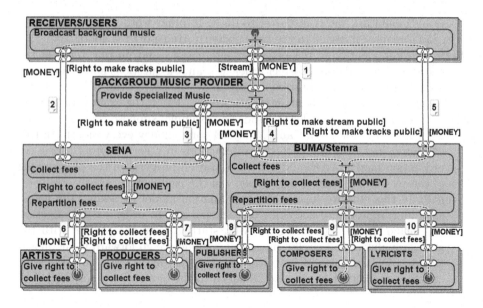

**Fig. 2.** Value model of providing music by Streaming

**IPR Societies:** IPR Societies perform mainly two roles; collecting fees for each played or copied track and repartitioning it to IPR owners. This fee is related with the public use of music (tracks). So, if an actor publicly provides music, it has to pay for the right of providing music.

**Right Owners:** Right owners are those who perform a specific track, i.e., play tracks, write lyrics, produce and publish tracks.

A BMP can provide background music in two ways. It can either deliver hard copies or a stream of tracks. Hard copies in this context are provided by a physical device in which a Receiver stores tracks provided by BMPs. On the other hand, a stream is a flow of tracks that the BMP delivers to a Receiver using Internet-based technology for direct playing. So, the main difference between these two ways of providing music is either allowing to store tracks at Receivers or not.

This main difference also generates two value models. If the BMP delivers hard copies, it must pay to IPR Societies which collect fees about replicating music, so making copies of tracks. Otherwise, when providing streams, the BMP must pay to IPR Societies which collect fees related with making a stream available to the public. Here we only investigate the second case (see figure 2).

To be able to provide music to the public, Receivers also have to pay IPR Societies. Paying BUMA/Stemra is about the copyright that the composer and/or lyricist holds, whereas paying SENA is related to the rights of the performing artists and producer. The process described so far is concerned with collecting fees. Therefore the next step is to repartition all those fees. SENA repartitions fees to Artists and Producers, and BUMA/Stemra does the same for Publishers, Composers and Lyricists.

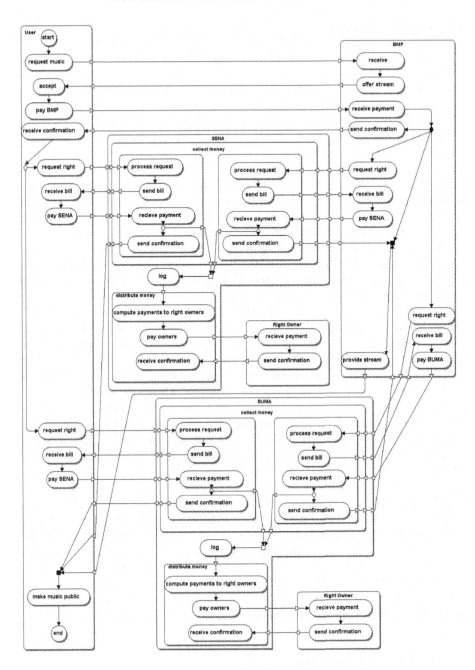

**Fig. 3.** Coordination model of providing music by Streaming

## 5.2   Coordination Model

We applied our simple method to this case. The result is shown in figure 3. According to step 1 of the proposed method, actors are the same in the corresponding models. Because of the space limitation and the high similarity that is between right owners, we only include one right owner representing all of them. Therefore actors are: *Receivers/Users, BMP, BUMA, SENA, and right owner.*

In step 2, that is the most fundamental step, we identify the necessary interactions for realizing the value transfers. Under the simplifying assumptions we include four interactions to realize each pair of value transfers (a value exchange). The most obvious ones in this value model (figure 2) are those tagged as numbers 2, 3, 4, and 5. In all these four cases we have a pair of value transfers (money and right) being exchanged between two partners. Therefore according to step 2, using a pair of request-reply interactions they can be realized.

The value exchange tagged as number 1, has a subtle difference with the proposed method. In this case the BMP sends back an extra confirmation to the Receiver/User. This extra confirmation is just for the sake of efficiency. If we remove this confirmation message, the Receiver/User has to wait until the arrival of the stream and after that do the necessary activities (payments), before being able to use the stream. The other value exchanges (numbers 6 through 10) are like *scheduled payments* described in step 2. Hence, we include only two interactions in to the coordination model to realize them.

We don't have the phenomenon of *third parties* thus we skip step 3. Step 4 is for putting the interactions in the correct order. Therefore, starting from the Receivers towards right owners we should find out the answers to the questions of this step regarding each value exchange and using the answers put the interactions in a correct order. Here we haven't consider the time constraints and durations because we suppose the provisioning of music as a simple service for which the duration is already determined. Also the way in which the payments are being done in real life depends on the situations and the agreements that have been made between payers and receivers. For example, one possible case is that BUMA and SENA pay the right owners in batch at the end of every month or so. But, here we consider only the simple case and leave considering all the details about payment methods and the cardinality or duration of the interactions to future work. In the last step we include the activities in the coordination model and using them connect the interactions to each other. We can also add details and other necessary activities. For example, for this particular case we could include the *log* as an additional activity in SENA and BUMA.

## 6   Analysis of Results

The proposed guidelines make a simple method that avoids complicated concepts like property right, physical delivery, etc. and still is able to guide the modeler to a coordination model that on face value is consistent with the value model. By applying our method on the above case study we learned that:

- The application of these guidelines will indeed lead to a coordination model.
- The obtained coordination model is valid in the following sense: A stake-holder who accepts the value model ("this is how we will earn money in this business web") will also accept the coordination model ("this is how we will coordinate our actions with other actors in order to realize the value model").

We still want to do the following in order to further validate and improve our method:

- Comparison with the other methods. We observe that the papers do not give enough information to apply those methods to the described case (the bits of missing information concerning those methods will be identified in future work). But we will in the future apply our own method to more cases, and report the results.
- Apply our method to more complex cases to test its general applicability.
- Define an integrated consistency concept and prove that our method delivers consistent models.

## 7   Conclusion and Future Work

In this paper we have discussed the problem of how to go from a business/value model to a coordination coordination model in a stepwise and systematic way. Thanks to the conceptual commonalities that exist between the two models, a method could be proposed that starts with a value model where the main actors and their relationships, in the form of value exchanges, are identified. In a number of steps each value exchange is analyzed and by answering specific questions a coordination model is designed. The coordination model represents the interactions and interdependencies between the cooperating parties in terms of exchanged messages. We consider a special collection of interactions to realize the value exchanges of value models.

Future research involves eliminating different simplification assumptions such as trust that we have made here in constructing the coordination model. Another topic for future research includes investigations on different paying methods and finding a comprehensive collection of the most common ones to be able to make some patterns for paying methods and go from one to the other automatically.

## Acknowledgments

The authors would like to thank the colleagues Anna Chmielowiec, Ivn S. Razo-Zapata, and Patricio de Alencar Silva in SENA case study. In particular, we thank Lianne Bodenstaff for her valuable contribution towards this work.

# References

1. Tapscott, D., Ticoll, D., Lowy, A.: Digital capital: harnessing the power of business webs. Ubiquity 1(13), 3 (2000)
2. Gordijn, J., Akkermans, H., van Vliet, H.: Business modelling is not process modelling. In: ER Workshops, pp. 40–51 (2000)
3. Gordijn, J., Akkermans, H.: Value Based Requirements Engineering: Exploring Innovative e-Commerce Ideas. Requirements Engineering Journal 8, 114–134 (2002)
4. Pijpers, V., Gordijn, J.: Consistency checking between value models and process models; a best-of-breed approach. Accepted at the BUSITAL (2008)
5. Zarvić, N., Wieringa, R., van Eck, P.: Checking the alignment of value-based business models and it functionality. In: SAC 2008: Proceedings of the 2008 ACM symposium on Applied computing, pp. 607–613. ACM, New York (2008)
6. Zlatev, Z., Wombacher, A.: Consistency between e3-value models and activity diagrams in a multi-perspective development method. In: Meersman, R., Tari, Z. (eds.) OTM 2005. LNCS, vol. 3760, pp. 520–538. Springer, Heidelberg (2005)
7. Bodenstaff, L., Wombacher, A., Reichert, M.U.: On formal consistency between value and coordination models. Technical Report TR-CTIT-07-91, Enschede (October 2007)
8. Bodenstaff, L., Wombacher, A., Reichert, M.U.: Dynamic consistency between value and coordination models - research issues. Technical Report TR-CTIT-06-50, Enschede (2006)
9. Pijpers, V., Gordijn, J.: Bridging business value models and process models in aviation value webs via possession rights. In: HICSS '07: Proceedings of the 40th Annual Hawaii International Conference on System Sciences, Washington, DC, USA, p. 175a. IEEE Computer Society, Los Alamitos (2007)
10. Andersson, B., Bergholtz, M., Grégoire, B., Johannesson, P., Schmitt, M., Zdvavkovic, J.: From business to process models–a chaining methodology. Conference paper (2006)
11. Wieringa, R., Pijpers, V., Bodenstaff, L., Gordijn, J.: Value-driven coordination process design using physical delivery models. In: Li, Q., Spaccapietra, S., Yu, E., Olivé, A. (eds.) ER 2008. LNCS, vol. 5231, pp. 216–231. Springer, Heidelberg (2008)
12. Wieringa, R., Gordijn, J.: Value-oriented design of correct service coordination processes: Correctness and trust. In: 20th ACM Symposium on Applied Computing, March 13-17, pp. 1320–1327. ACM Press, New York (2005)

# SOP$^4$EBPM: Generating Executable Business Services from Business Models*

Rubén de Juan-Marín[1] and Rubén Darío Franco[2]

[1] Instituto Tecnológico de Informática
Univ. Politécnica de Valencia, 46022 Valencia, Spain
rjuan@iti.upv.es
[2] Centro de Investigación, Gestión e Ingeniería de Producción
Univ. Politécnica de Valencia, 46022 Valencia, Spain
dfranco@cigip.upv.es

**Abstract.** This paper presents the vision considered by the REMPLANET project for providing a platform for the discovery, design, deployment, execution, interaction, operation, optimization and analysis of extended business processes with the objective of supporting the collaborative decision processes in the context of Resilient Multi-Plant Networks in the manufacturing sector.

**Keywords:** Business Process Management (BPM), Software Oriented Architectures (SOA), Collaborative Processes, Workflows.

## 1 Introduction

One of the main topics of research in the enterprise interoperability (EI) [1] field nowadays is the Business Process Management (BPM) [2], putting special emphasis in the interorganizational collaboration aspects. The main goal of BPM is to increase the effectiveness and efficiency of enterprises through the holistic management of their business processes. This holistic management includes modeling, automation, integration, monitoring and continuous improvement of processes as a way of providing high levels of quality. Among the different aspects involved in BPM, the direct translation from a business process business perspective representation of business processes to a technical process representation that can be executed (a.k.a. workflow) – automated – by a workflow technology [3], takes a lot of research effort. The idea consists in being able to obtain an abstract representation – workflow – taking as starting point a business perspective description in an automated and straightforward way. Moreover, in enterprise network scenarios this translation has to provide facilities for defining interoperable technical aspects that support the necessary level of co-operation among partners.

Most of traditional approaches concerning workflow automation have been focused on very clearly structured business process. However, this paper presents the vision that has been taken in the Resilient Multi-Plant Networks project (REMPLANET, http://www.remplanet.eu) where BPM concepts and methodologies will be applied to resilient

---

* This work has been funded by the 7th FP EU grant 229333.

R. Poler, M. van Sinderen, and R. Sanchis (Eds.): IWEI 2009, LNBIP 38, pp. 107–112, 2009.

manufacturing scenarios, where many heterogeneous partners needs be integrated and their processes be interconnected.

The intended approach will consist in defining a set of extensions and restrictions to follow in the traditional business process definition that will facilitate the generation of executable representations in a specific platform overcoming the gaps between both.

Therefore, with a single business process representation based on a business perspective, which can be easily defined by business analysts, the system will be able to obtain the executable representation supporting interorganizational collaboration. Thus, it will be only necessary to maintain a single representation, simplifying the business process management as a whole. The problem resides in the fact that usually a direct translation from a process business perspective representation leads to a workflow representation that presents some lacks which make it impossible to obtain all the expected benefits from its automated execution. This is due to the fact, that the existing models at both levels, and therefore their respective representations, have different goals as it has been explained in [4].

Business perspective process models are oriented to represent business processes in an easy, understandable and precise enough way for businesses experts, but not their automation. In fact, these representations help enterprises to: a) have a good knowledge and understanding of their processes, b) ensure the quality of their processes and, c) to facilitate the cooperation among different enterprises, helping to establish the interaction points amongst their respective processes. Technical aspects needed at execution time are out of the scope of this business modeling. Therefore, generating executable representations from these models is not enough.

Executable models, used for modeling workflows, as they should be executed automatically by software, in addition to the flow of activities and participant roles also have to define: a) repositories and sources of process related information and b) the way in which actors can participate in the automated execution for ensuring the progress and termination of the workflow. Actors represent both human and machine (e.g. processes) participants. This extra information should cover technical aspects for the automated workflow execution.

In order to obtain workflow representations rich enough to be executed in an automated way from business processes represented using a human readable model, it is necessary to enrich the original representations with extra information [4]. Besides, it is necessary that these business human readable representations can define precisely all necessary types of business collaboration in a network.

Moreover, the presented approach also considers the basic aspect of interoperability at workflow level [5], in order to facilitate the cooperation of members belonging to a resilient multi-plant network being necessary to obtain maximum benefits from collaboration. In doing so, the business processes are offered as services to the outside, promoting therefore the development of new business processes based on the composition or aggregation of existing ones.

This paper is structured as follows: in Section 2 an overview of the REMPLANET project and its main goals is presented. The environment for the SOP⁴EBPM is explained in Section 3. Some related work is detailed in Section 4. Finally, Section 5 presents some conclusions.

## 2   REMPLANET Project

This project is funded by the European Union through the 7th Framework Programme. Its main concept is the development of methods, guidelines and tools for the implementation of the Resilient Multi-Plant Networks Model in non-hierarchical manufacturing networks, characterized by non-centralized decision making.

The project considers that a resilient organization has the capability to respond rapidly to unforeseen change, even chaotic disruption. It is the ability to bounce back — and, in fact, to bounce forward — with speed, determination and precision. In recent studies, resilience is regarded as the next phase in the evolution of traditional, place-centric enterprise structures to highly virtualized, customer-centric structures that enable people to work anytime, anywhere. A resilient organization effectively aligns its strategy, operations, management systems, governance structure, and decision-support capabilities, so that it can uncover and adjust to continually changing risks, endure disruptions to its primary earnings drivers, and create advantages over less adaptive competitors. From an organizational point of view, the "resilience" concept has two fundamental perspectives: strategic resilience and operational resilience. On one hand the strategic resilience is not about responding to a one-time crisis, or just having a flexible supply chain. It is about continuously anticipating and adjusting to discontinuities that can permanently impair the value proposition of a core business. Strategic resilience refers, therefore, to a capacity for continuous reconstruction. On the other hand, operational resilience can be understood as the ability to respond to the ups and downs of the business cycle or to quickly rebalance product-service mix, processes, and the supply chain, by bolstering enterprise agility and flexibility in the face of changing environments.

In order to achieve these goals several models, guidelines, tools and platforms will be developed. So, the combination of all these elements will provide to networks of manufacturing enterprises a generic way for increasing their competitiveness in a more and more exigent, dynamic and globalised market.

Among these results it must be highlighted the development of an ICT platform for efficient real time collaborative planning/scheduling execution. Every future supply network member will be interconnected through this platform. The ICT platform incorporates interoperability functionalities, to facilitate the supply network member's systems integration, and allow each new member a fast connection to the network. Additional ICT platform functionalities will allow to handle customer's customized orders, or incidents that take place in the network, in a non-hierarchical and real-time decentralized decision making way. In both cases, the most suitable network configuration is established in order to increase feasibility and accuracy of customer service. In next section it is presented this platform.

## 3   REMPLANET SOP<sup>4</sup>EBPM

In the context of the REMPLANET project, the Service-Oriented Platform (SOP) for Extended Business Process Management (EBPM) will provide support for the collaborative work in a resilient network as it has been said before. The REMPLANET environment in which the SOP<sup>4</sup>EBPM will work is shown in Figure 1. On the sequel, the different elements composing this environment and how they interact in order to provide the maximum performance for the platform are described.

One of the challenges to face in the project is to select and validate the right combination of notations, languages, mappings and tools appropriate for the requirements of REMPLANET EBPM. Thus, it is necessary to review standard proposals of collaboration initiatives like ebXML [6], RosettaNet PIPs – Partner Inferface Process – [7], OAGIS [8] in order to select the most suitable approach for the initial extended process harmonization. The goal is to be able to define the appropriate level of interoperability in the resulting processes for supporting the collaboration in the Resilient Organization. This study will provide several Modeling Constructs that will be used in order to obtain the Collaborative Business Process Models necessary for the SOA[4]EBPM platform.

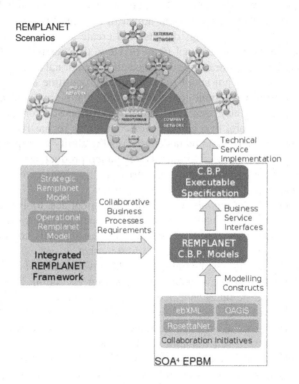

**Fig. 1.** REMPLANET SOP[4]EBPM Environment

The Integrated REMPLANET Framework will link the Strategic REMPLANET model and Operational REMPLANET model developed in the project context for obtaining the maximum benefits. On one hand, the former will provide tools, methods, and guidelines to enable enterprises to profit from open innovation along the entire multi-plant value network. On the other hand, the second will provide an Operational Resilient Supply Network Model, as well as its tools, methods, and guidelines to help globalised manufacturing organisations to decide where to buy-manufacture-assembly, and how to deliver, the different customized products demanded from different markets, as cheaply and as quickly as possible. Their combination within the Integrated REMPLANET Framework will provide and define the Business Processes that best fit the efficacy and efficiency requirements (see Fig 1).

So, the combination of collaborative modeling constructs and business processes requirements will allow the definition of Collaborative Business Process Models. These models will represent the collaborative business processes in a readable and understandable way for business analysts. Moreover, these models will be taken as inputs for generating the Collaborative Executable Representation using Business Service Interfaces as a way of introducing interoperability among the network members in the executable representation.

The next step in the REMPLANET SOP⁴EBPM environment process consists in implementing the necessary services (if they don't exist) in order to prepare the whole system for being operative. Once it has been done, the business process can be deployed among all the participants at different levels (company network, group network and external network) in order to be used in production. These obtained implementations will be deployed in the SOP⁴EPBM platform supporting their execution. The SOP⁴EPBM will provide support for the discovery, design, deployment, execution, interaction, operation, optimization and analysis of EBP with the objective of supporting the collaborative decision processes. Moreover, it will provide capabilities for services re-use and composition to support and create resilient and agile resource networks based on the SOA paradigm [9]. The design and implementation of the SOA⁴EBPM platform will be based on Open Source tools and will follow international standards.

## 4  Related Work

In regard to the coordination of the business perspective and the technical perspective, the paper [4] proposed two additional approaches to the Aspect Oriented Architecture: Layered Architecture and Domain Service Architecture. The Layered Architecture takes as starting point the technical process –workflow– and enriches it for obtaining the business perspective. This facilitates the separation among both perspectives but severe limitations are introduced due to synchronization problems. In the Domain Service Architecture technical and business aspects are encapsulated in modules, facilitating the isolation of technical details but depending on the selection of decomposition criteria. As the three presented architectures have different advantages and drawbacks they encouraged to combine these alternatives in order to maximize the advantages of the architectures.

Many proposals have appeared in last years in order to specify workflows and most of them have considered the necessity of workflow collaboration among enterprises. The authors of [5] presented a framework of requirements to consider for interorganizational workflows and compared several approaches considering the facilities they provided for defining these collaborative workflows. They observed how none of them supported correctly all the proposed requirements. Therefore, they proposed the option of extending existing languages or combining them.

## 5 Conclusions

In this paper it has been presented the vision of the REMPLANET project for obtaining a platform, SOP$^4$EBPM, that will support a fully non-centralized decision making process, as is expected to be achieved in non-hierarchical manufacturing networks. Complementary, this platform will enable dynamic and fast-responsive adaptation of IT-based organizational mechanisms needed to fully achieve the resilience structure that REMPLANET is proposing.

This platform will based on open standard tools and international standards will put a special emphasis in the collaborative business process modeling for Resilient Multi-Plant Networks of the manufacturing sector, and their corresponding translation to executable representations. Moreover, it will take advantage of interoperable services as a way of facilitating collaboration and coordination in the whole network context.

## References

1. Doumeingts, G., Müller, J., Morel, G., Vallespir, B. (eds.): Enterprise Interoperability: New Challenges and Approaches, XVI, 587, p. 185 (2007) ISBN: 978-1-84628-713-8
2. van der Aalst, W.M.P., ter Hofstede, A.H.M., Weske, M.: Business Process Management: A Survey. In: van der Aalst, W.M.P., ter Hofstede, A.H.M., Weske, M. (eds.) BPM 2003. LNCS, vol. 2678, pp. 1–12. Springer, Heidelberg (2003)
3. Leyman, F., Roller, D.: Production Workflow: Concepts and Techniques. Prentice-Hall, Englewood Cliffs (2000)
4. Henkel, M., Zdravkovic, J.: Architectures for Service-oriented Processes. In: Procedings of the Nordic Conference on Web Services (NCWS 2004), Växsjö, Sweden, November 22-23 (2004)
5. Bernauer, M., Kramler, G., Kappel, G., Retschitzegger, W.: Specification of Interorganizational Workflows - A Comparison of Approaches. In: Proceeding of the 7th World Multiconference on Systemics, Cybernetics and Informatics (SCI), Orlando, USA (2003)
6. Ebxml (May 2008), http://www.ebxml.org
7. Rowell, M.: OAGIS - A "Canonical" Business Language. White paper (2002)
8. Damodaran, S.: B2B integration over the Internet with XML: RosettaNet successes and challenges. In: International World Wide Web Conference, pp. 188–195 (2004)
9. Bieberstein, N., Bose, S., Fiammante, M., Jones, K., Shah, R.: Service-Oriented Architecture (SOA) Compass. IBM Press (2006)

# A Framework for a Decision Support System in a Hierarchical Extended Enterprise Decision Context

Andrés Boza, Angel Ortiz, Eduardo Vicens, and Raul Poler

Research Centre on Production Management and Engineering (CIGIP),
Universidad Politécnica de Valencia,
Camino de Vera s/n. Ed 8G – Esc. 4 – Nivel 1,
46022 – Valencia, Spain
{aboza,aortiz,evicens,rpoler}@cigip.upv.es

**Abstract.** Decision Support System (DSS) tools provide useful information to decision makers. In an Extended Enterprise, a new goal, changes in the current objectives or small changes in the extended enterprise configuration produce a necessary adjustment in its decision system. A DSS in this context must be flexible and agile to make suitable an easy and quickly adaptation to this new context. This paper proposes to extend the Hierarchical Production Planning (HPP) structure to an Extended Enterprise decision making context. In this way, a framework for DSS in Extended Enterprise context is defined using components of HPP. Interoperability details have been reviewed to identify the impact in this framework. The proposed framework allows overcoming some interoperability barriers, identifying and organizing components for a DSS in Extended Enterprise context, and working in the definition of an architecture to be used in the design process of a flexible DSS in Extended Enterprise context which can reuse components for futures Extended Enterprise configurations.

**Keywords:** Decision Support System, Extended Enterprise, Interoperability, Hierarchical Production Planning.

## 1 Introduction

The decision system allows to reach the stated objectives in the organizations. In order to provide the necessary information for decision-making, the information system becomes a key element within this decision making process. A Decision Support System (DSS), as a computer technology solution that can be used to support complex decision-making [1], relates to decision and information systems.

The increasing collaboration among enterprises during the entire product life cycle and constant changes in inter and intra organizational environment is a trend in the global market [2]. This is generating news inter-enterprise relationships like Extended Enterprise or Virtual Enterprise.

An Extended Enterprise is defined as the formation of closer coordination in the design, development, costing and the coordination of the respective manufacturing schedules of cooperating independent manufacturing enterprises and related suppliers [3]. Relationships between the participating enterprises are for a long term integration

R. Poler, M. van Sinderen, and R. Sanchis (Eds.): IWEI 2009, LNBIP 38, pp. 113–124, 2009.

and more stable than other configurations like Virtual Enterprise [4]. In this decision context, the decision process is more complex than inside a single organization and a DSS for an extended enterprise must consider these inter-dependencies [5]. Environment changes where organizations are becoming more complex yet more agile and flexible, and global regulatory, and competitive factors rapidly change, affecting the design and use of these tools [1].

On the other hand, the legacy software systems play a key role in any inter-organizational DSS. These legacy systems, located in the participating enterprises, are the main data source for the DSS. In this sense, ERP users highlight the importance of decision support and trans-organizational objectives in ERP planning.

This paper proposes a framework for a Decision Support System in a Hierarchical Extended Enterprise Decision Making (HEEDM) context. We make a hierarchical approach to this decision context, where the coordination between decision activities in strategic, tactical and operative levels is made according to a hierarchical structure. This means that each one will pursue its own goals, but always considering those of superior levels, on which they depend, and those of inferior levels, at which they restrict. We propose to extend the Hierarchical Production Planning structure to a HEEDM context. In this way, a framework is defined using components of Hierarchical Production Planning.

## 2 Hierarchical Production Planning

In the Hierarchical Production Planning (HPP) systems, the decisions are split in sub-problems. Each sub-problem is referred to a decision-making level in the organizational structure and an optimization model is constructed for solving each sub-problem. To ensure effective decision-making, a linkage must exist between these models at each hierarchical level and an adequate aggregation/disaggregation process of information between levels. The decisions that are taken in an upper level impose restrictions on lower decision levels. In response, the detailed decisions provide the necessary feedback to evaluate the quality of the decision. Each hierarchical level has its own characteristics, including length of the decision horizon, level of detail of the required information and forecast, scope of the decision, and type of manager in charge of executing the decision [6][7][8][9][10][11][12][13]. The utility to use this hierarchic approach in inter-enterprise systems appears in works as [13][14][15][16][17]. Some modeling frameworks provide a structured approach to model the decision system, e.g. the GRAI model divide the decision system into level of decision-making and can be used in to provide a methodology for the design of the hierarchical production planning systems [13].

The Information System is a key tool for the HPP systems and appears since the first works in HPP, by example, [6] include technical characteristics about procedures, functions, inputs and outputs in the computer. Others works in this area have also included information about the Information System [7][18][19][20][21][22][23][13][24][25].

## 3 Logical Constructs for Information and Decision Systems

According to the Principle of Graduated Flexibility: "A model's mathematical structure and detailed data should be represented and implemented in such a way that, over the lifetime of an application, the most commonly required model changes are the easiest to make, while less commonly required changes may be more difficult". The independency between model's mathematical structure and data allows defining DSS that solve these models for different data sets [26][27].

Data Modeling, Decision Modeling and Model Investigation, are logical constructs, which play a leading role both in the interaction of information systems and decision technologies, as well as in rational decision making [28]:

- Data Modeling refers to the 'structured' internal representation and external presentation of recorded facts. Broadly speaking this provides the decision-maker with information about their decision problem.
- Decision Modeling is the development of a model, or a range of models that captures the structure as well as the decisions in respect of a given problem. These models are used to evaluate possible decisions (actions) in a given problem domain, and the probable outcomes of these actions.
- Model Analysis and Investigation refers to the instantiation of the model with data, and the evaluation of the model parameters as well as the results in order to gain confidence and insight into the model.

Following this classification, we have made a framework for a DSS in HEEDM context with the necessary components for data modeling, decision modeling and model analysis and investigation.

## 4   A Framework for Decision Support Systems in Hierarchical Extended Enterprise Decision Making

This section is structured in four parts, firstly the components of the framework are defined, secondly, the relationships between components are explained, thirdly, the main roles needed to model and operate are identified, and finally a DSS platform is introduced.

### 4.1  Components

The components are defined for data modeling, decision modeling and model analysis and investigation.

The Data Modeling components included in this framework are defined in order to obtain a structured representation of the data used in a hierarchical extended enterprise decision making context. IDEF1 [29] and E-R Diagram [30] have been used to define these components. Each decision level works with a data set. The structured representation of these data sets, by means of entities, relation and attributes, for all decision models make up the data modeling.

The Decision Modeling components are defined in order to obtain a structured representation of hierarchical decision models. The hierarchy design process [13] has been employed to define these components.

On the other hand, the Model Analysis and Investigation components are defined in order to the instantiation of the models with data. Separation of Models from problems statements and solvers, and separation of general structure and instantiating data [26][28] have been utilized.

## Data Modeling

*Decision Data Model's Entity.* Represents the information maintained in organizations about physical or conceptual objects (e.g., people, places, things or ideas) and which appears in decision problems in hierarchical extended enterprise decision making (HEEDM). These elements can be described in a low or high abstraction level.

*Decision Data Model's Relation.* Represents an association between Decision Data Model's Entities or between instances of the same Entity.

*Decision Data Model's Attribute.* An attribute is a property or characteristic of a Decision Data Model's Entity or Relation. This is one element of information that is known about a particular Decision Data Model's Entity or Decision Data Model's Relation, and useful for a decision problem in HEEDM.

*Decision Data Model.* Subset of data model's entities, relations and attributes which are used in a single decision model. These decision data models will be instanced with data for a decision model in the Model Analysis and Investigation and will be associated with a Level Model inside the Hierarchy Level in a hierarchical extended enterprise decision.

## Decision Modeling

*Hierarchy.* Identifier of a hierarchical ordered set of decision problems in which a complex decision problem in an extended enterprise context is divided.

*Hierarchy Level.* Identifier of a level in the hierarchy. Each level has associate a decision sub-problem.

*Decision Model.* A mathematical representation of a decision problem to find the best solution. The decision model uses the entities, relations and attributes of the problem as index, data entries, decision or bounds variables for its definition, but not their values. The decision model will be associated with a Decision Data Model.

*Level Model.* A Decision Data Model and a Decision Model associate to a Hierarchy Level.

*Aggregation/ Disaggregation Process.* Each Level Model is treated at a certain degree of abstraction (e.g., products-families or machines-cells). The Aggregation/ Disaggregation Processes link information between lower and upper levels of a hierarchy.

## Model Analysis and Investigation

*Decision Context.* Identifier of a Decision Context. A hierarchy is appropriate in a particular setting which is necessary to identify. A hierarchy could be extrapolated to others decision contexts.

*Data Source.* Data bases, files or spreadsheets in organization information systems where the data of a Decision Data Model are located.

*Level Resolution Process.* Process to obtain Definitive Decision Data at a Level Model. This is a complex process in which others components have been identified. The following components are included in this process.

*Extract, Transformation and Load (ETL) Process of Data for a Level Model.* The data of the Decision Data Model associated to this Level Model are extracted, transformed and loaded from the Data Source to an Analytical Database. The Entities, Relationships and Attributes defined in the Decision Data Model are instancied from the Data Source and stored in an Analytical Database. This process uses the aggregation/disaggregation process in order to complete these Analytical Data. (e.g. an entity "worker" from the Decision Data Model is instanced in all workers from a Data Source –a company- to the Analytical Database)

*Analytical Data.* Data obtained from the Data Sources according to a Decision Data Model and an aggregation/disaggregation process. These Analytical Data are stored in the Analytical Database.

*Solver Process.* A resolution process, which is capable of understanding a Decision Model and processing a data set (Analytical Data) to produce results. The results obtained after its execution are the Decision Data.

*Decision Data.* Data obtained for the Solver Process after its execution with a set of Analytical Data for a Decision Model.

*Definitive Decision Process.* The process by which the decision-maker consider additional factors in order to make its definitive decision.

*Definitive Decision Data.* Data about the definitive decision taken by the decision-maker in a Level Model. Decision Data obtained by the solver can be updated by the decision-maker in function of their judgments and choices.

## 4.2 Relationships

The relationship between the components of the framework for a DSS in HEEDM context defined above is showed in figure 1.

Concerning the relationships between components in the data modeling, these exist between entities with their attributes, between entities with other entities and the attributes that arise, and the subgroups of these components that form a valid decision data modeling for a single decision model in a hierarchical extended enterprise decision making context.

Libraries of entities, relations and attributes valid for different Decision Data Models can be built. In this way, these components are re-usable for different decision models (e.g. in a hierarchy, an entity can be used in several decision model, or in different hierarchies, this entity can be used with other extended enterprise configuration using the same or new attributes).

Concerning the relationships between components in the decision modeling, these exist between the hierarchies defined with its levels (each hierarchy can have a different

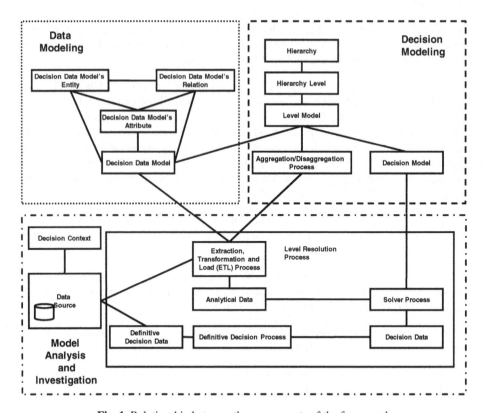

**Fig. 1.** Relationship between the components of the framework

number of levels). Also, each hierarchy level has associated a decision sub-problem in the level model. This level model encloses the Decision Data Model and the Decision Model necessary to solve a decision sub-problem. Moreover, aggregation/ disaggregation processes are associated with a Level Model to link information between lower and upper levels in a Hierarchy.

In this case also, it is possible to create libraries of Decision Models valid for different Hierarchies.

Finally, concerning the relationships between components in the Model Analysis and Investigation, the Level Resolution Process is used to solve a decision sub-problem in an extended enterprise Decision Context. The Data Source in an extended enterprise decision context must be identified in order to Extract, Transform and Load all data necessary to instance the Decision Data Model. Analytical Data are obtained from this instantiation and completed with data obtained from the aggregation/disaggregation processes. The Solver Process use these Analytical Data for the resolution of a Decision Model and Decision Data are obtained. The decision-maker considers this information and additional factors in order to make a definitive decision (Definitive Decision Process). This Definitive Decision Data can be included in the Data Sources of participating enterprises.

## 4.3  Roles

We have defined the main roles needed to model and operate this DSS. The roles identified are:

**Table 1.** Roles and Tasks

| Role | Task |
|---|---|
| Decision-Maker | Person(s) in charge of a decision making for a certain level in a decision problem hierarchy. |
| Decision Model Designer | Person(s) in charge of constructing the suitable Decision Models for each level. |
| Information System Designer | Person(s) in charge of constructing the suitable Information System to give service to the information necessities |

In an extended enterprise context is necessary to assign these roles between the participating enterprises. The tasks assigned to each role will be detailed in the next section.

## 4.4  DSS Platform

To perform a HEEDM supported by a DSS is necessary to develop a software tool. This tool can be developed to be used in different HEEDM contexts. Once the tool will be built, a parameterization and customization to a particular HEEDM context is required. The defined roles must participate in this parameterization and customization process to configure, in an easy way, the DSS platform.

The extended enterprise have usually at the heart of its organization a large final assembly plant or a service company procured by its suppliers (1st tier supplier, 2nd tier supplier) and serviced by its engineering units, sales units, banks, etc. [4], this main organization must encourage to the other extended enterprise participating to built and use this DSS Platform.

### Built a DSS Platform
This platform must include the Data Model, Decision Model and Model Analysis and Investigation constructors of the hierarchical models (Fig. 2), that is, this platform must allow to include information about the structural components in a hierarchy. Also, the Aggregation/ Disaggregation Process, Extract, the Transformation and Load (ETL) Process, Solver Process or Definitive Decision Process can be included in this platform or can be outside but linked to this platform. To locate the process outside the platform can increase the flexibility if it is possible to change or adapt this process in an easier way.

A variety of software visions with interoperability orientation can be used in its implementation: Plug and Play Business Software [31], an integrated, unificated or federated structure [32], the implementation of the interoperability framework [33], the design of Decision Support System for Extended Enterprise [5], the information repository [34] or the Enterprise Model Management [35].

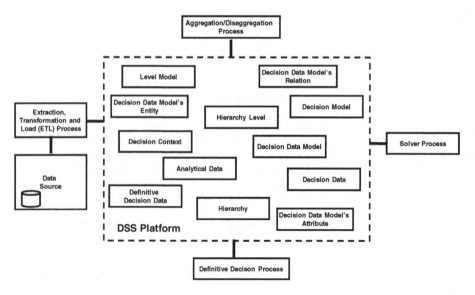

**Fig. 2.** DSS Platform

### Use of the DSS Platform for Modeling and Operations

*Modeling.* Decision makers must use the platform to include information about a new hierarchy. Information about the Decision Data Model and the Decision Model for this hierarchy must be incorporated in the platform.

Decision Model Designer helps the Decision Maker in order to make the suitable Decision Models for each level in the hierarchy, the aggregation/disaggregation process and decide the solver process to use.

Information System Designer helps the Decision Maker to connect the DSS Platform with the Data Sources with the Extraction, Transformation and Load (ETL) Process and connect the DSS Platform with the other process (Aggregation/Disaggregation Process, Solver Process and Definitive Decision Process).

*Operations.* Only the Decision Maker in each level uses the DSS Platform to obtain results and decide yours definitive decision. The components included in the model analysis and investigation are used to operate with them to obtain Definitive Decision Data. The DSS Platform must manage these components and launch the necessary processes.

*Remodeling.* A new goal, changes in the current objectives, or small changes in the extended enterprise configuration, produce a necessary adjustment in the DSS. Depending on the type of change will be necessary only the decision maker participation, or Decision Model Designer and/or Information System Designer for more complex changes.

*Simulations.* Simulation scenarios can be used by the decision makers when they define fictitious hierarchies where they can play with real (or fictitious) organizational data and use different decision models.

## 5 Interoperability Aspects

The proposed framework for a Decision Support System in a hierarchical extended enterprise decision context impacts into some interoperability aspects: enterprise levels, interoperability barriers and maturity models.

Although an extended enterprise context must have some interoperability characteristics solved, we approached these aspects from a general point of view.

The interoperability is achieved if the interaction between two enterprise systems can take place at various enterprise levels: data, services, processes and business [4]. The proposed framework includes: 1) the interoperability of data, in order to find and sharing information from heterogeneous data sources. 2) the interoperability of services, composing and making various application functions together. 3) the interoperability of processes which is limited to decision processes, and not other kind of processes; and 4) the interoperability of business where is necessary to harmonize the inter-enterprise decision making process in a hierarchical mode.

About the interoperability barriers (conceptual, organizational and technological) [36] (Fig. 3). Conceptual barriers related to the problems of syntactic and semantic of

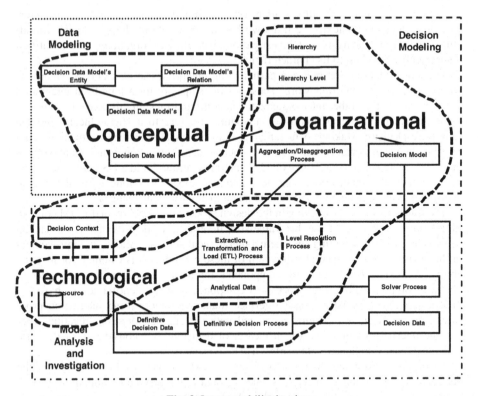

**Fig. 3.** Interoperability barriers

information to be exchanged appears in the Data Modeling. Organizational barriers related to the definition of responsibilities and authority so that interoperability can take place under good conditions appears in the Decision Modeling, specifically in the hierarchy definition, levels, decision models and aggregation/disaggregation processes, also appears in the Decision Context as a particular setting which is necessary to identify and, finally appears in the Definitive Decision Process in order to identify the decision maker who make the definitive decision. And Technological barriers appears mainly in the Extraction, Transformation and Load Processes where the decision context include one, two or n data sources. This framework allows to identify and organize components to overcoming interoperability barriers and reuses these components for futures configurations.

With reference to the degree of integration of the considered enterprises, in [37] are identified some maturity models such as LISI, LCIM, OIM or EIF. In order to carry out a HEEDM supported by a DSS, it is necessary to reach the necessary integration level of the maturity models for each shared decision process.

## 6  Conclusions

The proposed framework allows identifying components for a DSS in an inter-enterprise decision context. The framework structure (Data modeling, Decision modeling, and Model analysis and investigation) has allowed organizing the identified components according to its characteristics.

The close relationships between participating enterprises in an extended enterprise are a key factor in this framework. These relationships are for a long term integration and more stable than other inter-organizational configurations. In this context is possible to extent the Hierarchical Production Planning structure to a Hierarchical Extended Enterprise Decision Making. A hierarchical inter-organizational decision making is not possible between organization without conceptual, organizational and technological links. The more stable context in extended enterprise allows build a DSS with the necessary conceptual, organizational and technological links for a long term hierarchical decision making, but flexible and agile to adapt to environment changes.

The framework allows working in the design process of a DSS in a HEEDM context. In this sense, it is possible use this framework in order to made a flexible DSS that can be used in a variety of settings in where a hierarchical approach allows an improvement in the decision making. The identification of these components is essential for its reusability. A flexible DSS can reuse components for futures configurations. In order to obtain a comprehensible framework with components easily identifiable, we have not include other factors like the user inferface (data presentations and interaction processes), the consistency problems associated with the aggregation/disaggregation process, the interval of time after which the set of decisions is reconsidered, or database structures (data warehouse, data marts, OLAP and so on).

A DSS in an extended enterprise decision context can increase the flexibility of the decision making in these enterprises where global regulatory and competitive factors rapidly change. Using this framework, a DSS can be designed to be parameterized and customized in an easy way for different context with reusable decision models and data access.

An extended enterprise decision process implies communication and transactions between the participate enterprises, this paper review some interoperability aspects which impact in the proposed framework. In an HEEDM the interoperability barriers need to be overcome and this framework helps in this objective.

# References

1. Shim, J.P., Warkentin, M., Courtney, J.F., Power, D.J., Sharda, R., Carlsson, C.: Past, present, and future of decision support technology. Decision Support System 33, 111–126 (2002)
2. Chen, D., Doumeingts, G.: European initiatives to develop interoperability of enterprise applications - basic concepts, framework and roadmap. Annual Reviews in Control 27, 153–162 (2003)
3. Jagdev, H.S., Browne, J.: The extended enterprise - a context for manufacturing. Production Planning & Control 9(3), 219–229 (1998)
4. Chen, D., Doumeingts, G., Vernadat, F.: Architectures for enterprise integration and interoperability: Past, present and future. Computers in Industry 59, 647–659 (2008)
5. Zolghadri, M., Lecompte, T., Bourrieres, J.P.: Design of Decision Support Systems for Extended Enterprise. Studies In Informatics And Control With Emphasis on Useful Applications of Advanced Technology 11 (2002)
6. Hax, A., Meal, H.C.: Hierarchical Integration of Production Planning and Scheduling. Sloan Working Papers, pp. 656–673. ed. MIT, Cambridge (1973)
7. Bitran, G.R., Hax, A.C.: On the design of hierarchical production planning systems. Decision Science 8, 28–55 (1977)
8. Meal, H.C.: Putting Production Decisions Where They Belong. Harvard Business Review, Boston 62(2), 102–112 (1984)
9. Bitran, G.R., Tirupati, D.: Hierarchical Production Plannig. In: Graves, S.C., et al. (eds.) Handbooks in OR&MS, vol. 4. Elsevier Science Publishers B.V., Amsterdam (1993)
10. McKay, K.N., Safayeni, F.R., Buzacott, J.A.: A Review of Hierarchical Production Planning and its Applicability for Modern Manufacturing. Production Planning & Control 6, 384–394 (1995)
11. Vollmann, T.E., Berry, W.L., Whybark, D.C.: Sistemas de Planificación y Control de la Fabricación. IRWIN, Madrid (1995)
12. Schneeweiss, C.: Hierarchical Planning in Organizations: Elements of a general theory. International Journal of Production Economics 56, 547–556 (1998)
13. Vicens, E., Alemany, M.E., Andrés, C., Guarch, J.J.: A design and application methodology for hierarchical production planning decision support systems in an enterprise integration context. International Journal of Production Economics 74, 5–20 (2001)
14. Yan, H.: An interaction/prediction approach to hierarchical production planning and control with delay interaction. Computer Integrated Manufacturing Systems 10(4), 309–320 (1997)
15. De Kok, A.G., Fransoo, J.C.: Planning supply chain operations: Definition and comparison of planning concepts. In: Handbook in Operations Research and Management Science. Design and Analysis of Supply Chains, vol. 11. North-Holland, Amsterdam (2003)
16. Hurtubise, S., Olivier, C., Gharbi, A.: Planning tools for managing the supply chain. Computers & Industrial Engineering 46, 763–779 (2004)
17. Alix, T., Zolghadri, M., Bourrieres, J.: A decision support system for production and procurement planning of enterprises X-networks. In: IEEE International Conference on Systems, Man and Cybernetics, vol. 5, pp. 4371–4376 (2004)

18. Doumeingts, G., Pun, L., Mondain, M., Breuil, D.: Decision-making systems for production control planning and scheduling. International Journal of Production Research 16(2), 137–152 (1978)
19. Lario, F.C., Vicens, E.: Integrated System of MRP II Matriz-Based Hierarchical Planning: Its Computerized Implantation. In: Databases for Production Management. Elsevier Science Publishers, North-Holland (1990)
20. Davis, W.J., Thompson, S.D.: Production Planning and Control Hierarchy using a Generic Controller. IIE Transactions 25(4), 26–44 (1993)
21. Tsubone, H., Matsuura, H., Kimura, K.: Decision Support System for production planning –Concept and prototype. Decision Support Systems 13, 207–217 (1995)
22. Artiba, A., Aghezzaf, E.H.: An architecture of a multi-model system for planning and scheduling. International Journal of Computer Integrated Manufacturing 10(5), 380–393 (1997)
23. Wezel, W., Jorna, R.J.: The SEC-system reuse: support for scheduling system development. Decision Support Systems 26, 67–87 (1999)
24. Alemany, M.E.: Metodología y Modelos para el Diseño y Operación de los Sistemas de Planificación Jerárquica de la Producción. Aplicación a una Empresa del Sector Cerámico, PhD, Universidad Politécnica de Valencia (2003)
25. Boza, A.: Propuesta de un Sistema de Información de Ayuda para la Toma de Decisiones en Planificación Jerárquica de la Producción, PhD, Universidad Politécnica de Valencia (2006)
26. Geoffrion, A.M., Maturana, S.: Generating optimization-based decision support systems. In: 28th Hawaii International Conference on System Sciences, vol. 3, pp. 439–448 (1995)
27. Makowski, M.: A Structured Modeling Technology. EJOR, Feature Issue on Advances in Complex System Modeling 166(3), 615–648 (2005)
28. Dominguez-Ballesteros, B., Mitra, G., Lucas, C., Koutsoukis, N.-S.: Modelling and solving environments of mathematical programming (MP): a status review and new directions. Journal of the Operation Research Society 53, 1072–1092 (2002)
29. Mayer, R.: IDEF1 Information Modeling. Knowledge Based Systems, Inc., College Station, Texas (1992)
30. Chen, P.: The entity-relationship model-toward a unified view of data. ACM Transactions on Database Systems 1(1), 9–36 (1976)
31. Jacobson, A., Davidsson, P.: An Analysis of Plug and Play Business Software. Department of Systems and Software Engineering, Blekinge Institute of Technology (BTH) Ronneby, Sweden. Springer, Boston (2007)
32. ISO 14258. Industrial automation systems - concepts and rules for enterprise models, TC 184/SC5/WG1, Geneva, Switzerland (1999)
33. Campos, C., Martí, I., Grangel, R., Mascherpa, A., Chalmeta, R.: A Methodological Proposal for the Development. In: Proceedings of MDISIS, pp. 47–57 (2008)
34. Sheth, A., Kalinichenko, L.: Information Modeling in Multidatabase Systems: Beyond Data Modeling of an Interoperability Framework. In: Finin, T.W., Yesha, Y., Nicholas, C. (eds.) CIKM 1992. LNCS, vol. 752. Springer, Heidelberg (1993)
35. Goul, M., Corral, K.: Enterprise model management and next generation decision support. Decision Support Systems 43, 915–932 (2007)
36. Daclin, N., Chen, D., Vallespir, B.: Methodology for Enterprise Interoperability. In: Proceedings of the 17th World Congress The International Federation of Automatic Control, Seoul, Korea (2008)
37. Panetto, H.: Towards a Classification Framework for Interoperability of Enterprise Applications. International Journal of CIM 20(8), 727–740 (2007)

# An Interoperability Architecture for Networked Service Delivery

Stephan Kassel[1], Christian-Andreas Schumann[1], Andreas Rutsch[1],
and Thomas Reich[2]

[1] Westsächsische Hochschule Zwickau, Institute for Management and Information,
PSF 201037, 08012 Zwickau, Germany
{Stephan.Kassel,Christian.Schumann,Andreas.Rutsch}@fh-zwickau.de
[2] Neustädter-Forum Thomas Reich, Am Lederwerk 1, 07806 Neustadt/ Orla, Germany
reich.thomas@web.de

**Abstract.** This paper describes a service architecture which is especially suited for networked enterprises to provide services cooperatively. The overall architecture is described as well as the service composition process. The architecture is evaluated from a business perspective and the advantages and disadvantages are discussed.

**Keywords:** Service interoperability, interoperability architecture, business service composition, negotiation of services, quality of services.

## 1 Introduction

Service industry is gaining more and more attention in the USA and the European Union. [1] There are mainly three reasons for this development. First of all, labor costs for production are too high in Europe and the USA to be competitive any longer when concentrating on basic production. Second, the role of services is growing even in industry, thus leading to an increasing share of product-accompanying services on the overall value of the product. This leads to growing revenues for the companies who are performing well in defining that kind of enriched product offering. Third, the average age of the population of most of the European countries is ever-growing, leading to customers who are less in need for new products, but far more in need for special services in the health sector, medical treatment, nursing and personal care as well as everyday services.

So the business is in a dramatic transformation, leading to new chances for enterprises which are performing well in delivering those services, but also to harder constraints for enterprises which are not able to master this transformation.

With a deeper look at the service industry, it is possible to differentiate between basic services, which can be performed without a special qualification (we can call them low-level services), and very sophisticated services which can only performed by specialists with a high qualification (hereafter called high-level services). In the low-level service market, there is a big competition with the main constituent of the price of the service. This leads to shrinking revenues for the companies providing those low-level services, and to a tendency of off-shoring those services (if possible)

R. Poler, M. van Sinderen, and R. Sanchis (Eds.): IWEI 2009, LNBIP 38, pp. 125–132, 2009.

to low-salary regions of the world, where they could be performed with less costs for the service-providing companies and the customers of the services. In the high-level service market the competition is based on differentiation of the offering. This differentiation is achieved by the uniqueness of the service offering and/or the high quality of the service provisioned.

Especially these high-level services are becoming more and more complex, being constituted by a huge set of service primitives, which are combined in a special manner to provide the high-quality service offering specific for the customer.

Winners of this business are the enterprises who are able to provide these rich services to their customers. Competitive advantages can be achieved by building up networks of service providing specialists who are able to jointly deliver high-quality services. In this situation, technology is needed to help in the service composition, service qualification, and the service provisioning.

## 2 State of the Art

To achieve the goal of the paper, this section concentrates on the state of the art in the service composition, service provisioning, and service quality. The proposed architecture should solve the problems arising on these topics; therefore there is a concentration on the state of the art in the decision theory, helping to solve the problem of service composition, and on service interoperability, which helps on the service provisioning and the service quality.

### 2.1 Service Composition

The idea of combination of services out of basic service constituents is already widely used by service-oriented architectures (SOA) [2]. With SOA, it is possible to technically include services, which can be defined, provisioned, and billed at another place of the world. The services are usually provided on the Internet, by using special protocols to locate, and use service components. These service components consist mainly of software, but the basic SOA definition could easily be enhanced to other services which are not consisting of software alone. The composition of the services is mostly done by building business process models where the services, which should be used by some providers in the Internet, are explicitly named and some constraints on these services are defined, helping to identify the appropriate service on run-time of the business processes.

The service providers can be located anywhere in the world. The actual identification of the appropriate services at run-time is done by world-wide lookup in a repository of service descriptions, which are written in a formal kind of service pattern (WSDL) [3]. This mechanism is very useful for the composition of primitive basic services, but it totally lacks the ability to build up networks of corporations working together to provide first-class services on a high level to some common customers. The lookup of the services is mainly done by a service signature; there is little additional information on the service providers. So there is little information to help with the choice between different service providers. There is a need to use higher levels of support for the choice of the most appropriate service providers. This can be achieved by using decision aiding systems [4]. These kinds of systems are assisting in making rational decisions. They are not trying to automatically choose service providers. The decisions of choosing and combining services should have a simple yet powerful model based on some common economic methodologies. This provides a solution to the identification and combination problem of services. The decision aiding system should

- provide a negotiation aid on the business level,
- explicitly include business interoperability,
- provide a basic pricing model for the service constituents,
- show a simple interface to the customer shielding the complexity of the service provisioning from the customer, but at the same time provide a full choice including a rich set of services,
- model user requirements which can be helpful when there is a need for re-negotiation of the services consumed in case of a necessary mediation,
- explicitly address interoperability.

## 2.2 Service Provisioning

To provide a complex set of services, there is a need to match the requirements of the customers to several service providing companies. This leads to an interoperability problem, because there is no common understanding on the definition of the services, the context of the services, and the way of providing the service to this special customer. There is already a wide set of literature in the area of interoperability (e.g. [4], [5], [6], or [7]), but most publications still concentrate on technical levels of interoperability. Only in the latest time, there are some first research efforts on service interoperability, which has a different focus than the (technical) definition of service-oriented architectures (SOA). SOA concentrates on low-level, automated, technical-oriented services. The business-oriented terms of service industries, on the contrary, are defining services as immaterial "products". This has to be understood well inside of the IT-industry. In the roadmap of interoperability research of the European Union [8] there is a distinction of the technical interoperability levels from the business level of interoperability.

There is some research done in the enterprise interoperability scientific community, which can be useful for the definition of high-quality service interoperability. The work on model-driven interoperability, like [9], [10] and [11], provides some opportunities for an enhancement to service interoperability. There are some models of service interoperability existing, (e.g. [12] and [13]), which are very useful as a fundamental basis to solve the choice and combination problem. However, these models are rather complicated and lack simplicity in the practical usage. Severe problems, which are typical for service interoperability, are discussed in [14].

## 2.3 Service Quality

There is some work done to define service quality for the context of service interoperability. Especially the work on SQFD [15] shows, how some common models of service quality [16] can be enhanced to be used in the context of different service providers and different service consumers.

But there are some hard restrictions to these models, coming from a lack of common understanding on the nature of services at all. There are no common definitions of service standards, so the service providers and the service customers are individually defining their own model of the "ideal" service. This often leads to unsolved conflicts in provisioning of the services. The extent of the problem may be best seen by the statistics on failed software projects (a very special kind of services), which are talking about numbers of 24 % failed and 44 % challenged projects [17] leading to enormous economic losses.

There is a big need for pragmatic ways of solving these problems of service quality and resulting re-negotiations of the service goals and measures, which should be addressed in the architecture proposed by the author in the next section.

## 3    Components of the Service Architecture

The authors have proposed a business architecture for service interoperability [18]. The main components of this architecture are sketched in Figure 1. (For a complete description of the architecture, cf. [19]).

The highest level of the architecture consists of a set of business service classes, forming the service portfolio of the (networked) company. The customers of the service can choose from the different service classes, and are able to get individual service portfolios which are exactly suited to their needs.

In each business, there is a set of standard service classes, from which the customers are choosing. Especially high-level service providers are able to deliver a great variety of instatiations for those service classes. To provide a simple yet powerful way of presentation for the choice of the individual services, they are combined to decision trees, helping the customer to take a choice in a very limited time. In these decision trees, the services directly provided by the service company are listed near the services of the network partners. For the customer, the service portfolio is at that step of service choice transparent. There is a possibility that there are competitive services in this architecture, but there are clear rules defined, in which case which of these competitive services will be chosen. These rules are manifesting themselves in the decision trees. The task of the networked service company lies in the definition of the service classes, and the choice of the business partners in the service network and their responsibilities.

The composition of services is done on the third level of the service architecture, where the different services which are chosen, are combined by the combination of the service process models into some kind of skeleton service process.

In case of software services, these services can be easily provided by model transformation of the service processes to workflow models, which may be compiled to efficient code. In case of personal services, the workflows can be used to generate service provision orders to the people who are involved in the provision of the service.

The quality of the service is defined by the satisfaction of the customer with the service provisioning. There are a huge number of influencing factors when customer satisfaction is measured. Especially when the quality of complex services is evaluated, there are two big classes of these factors. The first class consists of the quality of

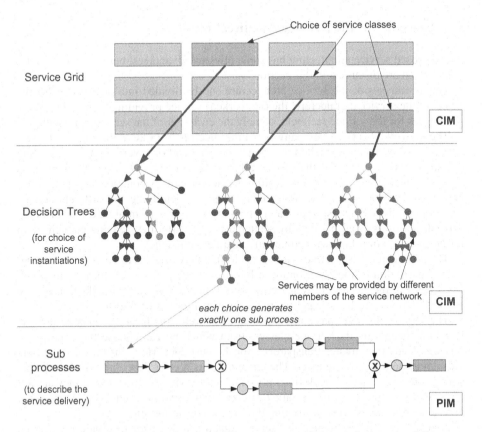

**Fig. 1.** The upper levels of the interoperability architecture for networked service delivery

the service components, which are mainly influenced by the choice of the right persons delivering the individual service, the choice of the right process steps and the pricing of the service which should be fair for the customer. There are additional constraints, like the timeliness of the service provision, which are influencing the evaluation of the individual service from the point of view of the customer. But there are other factors stemming from the complex service composition out of single services. They are mainly influenced by the composability of the service components. This means that the processes of the service components have to be seamlessly integrated. The customer is expecting that information he provides, is transferred along the overall service process, so the knowledge of the customer has to be provided from the service partners to each other. The customer does not want to explain his ideas more than once, he does not want to suffer from a distributed service provision, and he does not want to pay for transaction costs stemming from interoperability problems of the service-providing companies. The customer wants to have an impression of the services coming "from one hand", including a common timeline for all individual service components.

## 4   Discussion of the Service Architecture

The proposed service architecture has some obvious advantages, but also some limitations, which are discussed in this section.

The advantages of the service architecture can be divided into advantages for the owner of the service architecture, the (networked) service providing company, and the advantages for the service recipient, namely the customer of the service company.

The networked service company is getting much help in the definition of the services. The services are modelled in a pragmatic way and on a very high level, leading to a high-level overview of the service offering. This overview helps in negotiations with prospective service partners, leading to clearer partner contracts and more integrated service portfolios. The architecture helps in identifying the different service partners and their responsibilities and opens up measures to minimize risk of being dependent from special partners by scattered partner offerings, leaving enough room for business relationships with competitive partner companies.

The architecture also defines clear rules for the networked service provisioning, by a fixed definition of the partitioning of business. Each partner is informed, in which cases his offering is chosen by the customers. This may increase satisfaction for the business partners (if they are getting revenues out of the cooperation).

The service customer has some advantages as well. The clear structure of the service components by the service classes, from which he can choose the appropriate services, leads to a greater transparency for the customer. He is informed on the service components, he can expect. The customer gets a clear description of his choice, which could be enhanced with fixed prices for the service components, if they are not too complex. This is leading to target pricing for the services, thus the customer can give some price constraints restricting the service choice for him.

And if there are problems with service quality, it is easier to divide the service components which are problematic from the point of view of the customer, and replace them by other service components, which have similar properties, and may be better suited to the customer. Due to the pricing model which is pricing the individual components, it is easier to compromise on compensation for the work already done by the service provider, and the time invested by the service customer. This leads to a solution-oriented discussion about the conflicts in the service provisioning, and following to a higher satisfaction of both the customer and the service provider.

The architecture still shows some open issues which are not addressed now. First of these, there is no explicit description of company politics. But these politics always plays an important role in reality. There are often partnerships in service provisioning with companies, which are interesting from strategical reasons like being a key to an important future customer, or having other partners themselves, which are interesting from the view of the service company building up the network. These political partnerships cannot be modelled in an adequate manner. Second, the company building up the decision trees, is dividing the market share on the service revenues from the customers. It is hard to find objective choice criteria for the decision trees, especially when building a network with competing partners with very similar service offerings. Third, the compatibility of the services is dependant on some standardization on the interface description for the individual service processes. But this leads to some common black-box views of services. In this area, there is still a great need for research to define these standard service repositories.

## 5 Conclusion

In this paper, an architecture is defined, which is suitable for service composition. The advantages are described, as well as the open issues which should be solved to help for becoming a standard architecture for service interoperability. The authors are convinced that this kind of standardization is needed for service industry, especially when enterprises are operating on a global market with a big competition in the delivery of services. The networking aspects of service delivery are relevant competitive factors for service companies, so they need robust, pragmatic approaches to define these networks and their own role as well as the role of their network partners.

## References

1. OECD Stat Extracts, Online Database of the Organization for Economics Co-Operation and Development, `http://stats.oecd.org/`
2. Erl, T.: Service-oriented architecture: concepts, technology, and design. Prentice-Hall, Upper Saddle River (2006)
3. W3C, Web Services Description Language (WSDL) 1.1,
   `http://www.w3.org/TR/wsdl.html`
4. Tsoukiàs, A.: From decision theory to decision aiding methodology. European Journal of Operational Research 187, 138–161 (2008)
5. Doumeingts, G., Müller, J.P., Morel, G., Vallespier, B.: Enterprise Interoperability: New Challenges and Approaches. Springer, Berlin (2007)
6. Gonçalvez, J., Müller, J.P., Mertins, K., Zelm, M.: Enterprise Interoperability //: New Challenges and Approaches. Springer, London (2007)
7. Mertins, K., Ruggaber, R., Popplewell, K., Xu, X.: Enterprise Interoperability III: New Challenges and Industrial Approaches. Springer, London (2008)
8. Li, M.-S., Cabral, R., Doumeingts, G., Popplewell, K.: Enterprise Interoperability research roadmap (July 2006),
   `http://cordis.europa.eu/ist/ict-ent-net/ei-roadmap_en.htm`
9. Girard, P., Doumeingts, G.: GRAI-Engineering: a method to model, design and run engineering design departments. International Journal of Computer Integrated Manufacturing 17(8), 716–732 (2004)
10. Blanc, S., Ducq, Y., Vallespir, B.: Evolution management towards interoperable supply chains using performance measurement. Computers in Industry 58(7), 720–732 (2007)
11. Mertins, K., Knothe, T., Jäkel, F.-W.: Interoperability – Network Systems for SMEs. In: [7], pp. 511–520
12. Protogeros, N., Tektonidis, D., Mavridis, A., Wills, C., Koumpis, A.: FUSE: A Framework to Support Services Unified Process. In: [7], pp. 209–220
13. Xu, X.F., Mo, T., Wang, Z.J.: SMDA: A Service Model Driven Architecture. In: [6], pp. 291–302
14. Wang, Z., Xu, X.: Ontology-based Service Component Model for Interoperability of Service Systems. In: [7], pp. 367–380

15. Liu, S., Xu, X., Wang, Z.: A SQFD Approach for Service System Design Evaluation and Optimization. In: Proc. of I-ESA China 2009, pp. 23–27. IEEE Computer Society, Los Alamitos (2009)
16. Hauser, J.R., Clausing, D.: The House of Quality. Harvard Business Review, 63–73 (May-June 1988)
17. The Standish Group: CHAOS Summary 2009,
    http://www.standishgroup.com/index.php
18. Kassel, S.: Design of Services as Interoperable Systems. In: van Sinderen, M., Johnson, P., Kutvonen, L. (eds.) Proc. of IWEI 2008, pp. 58–62. CTIT proceedings, Twente (2008)
19. Kassel, S.: An Architectural Approach for Service Interoperability. In: Proc. of I-ESA China 2009, pp. 212–218. IEEE Computer Society, Los Alamitos (2009)

# Author Index

Aliee, Fereidoon Shams 52

Boza, Andrés 113
Buckl, Sabine 66

Campos, Cristina 38
Carrez, Cyril 1
Chalmeta, Ricardo 38
Chen, David 13

Daniele, Laura M. 25
de Juan-Marín, Rubén 107
Del Grosso, Enrico 1
Di Nitto, Elisabetta 80
Duque, Arantxa 38

Fatemi, Hassan 94
Franco, Rubén Darío 107

Gu, Qing 80

Jiménez-Ruiz, Ernesto 38
Johnson, Pontus 13

Karacan, Ömer 1
Kassel, Stephan 125

Lago, Patricia 80

Matthes, Florian 66

Ortiz, Angel 113

Pires, Luís Ferreira 25
Poler, Raul 113

Razavi, Mahsa 52
Reich, Thomas 125
Rutsch, Andreas 125

Schumann, Christian-Andreas 125
Schweda, Christian M. 66
Silva, Eduardo 25

Taglino, Francesco 1

Ullberg, Johan 13

van Sinderen, Marten 25, 94
Vicens, Eduardo 113

Wieringa, Roel 94